The Clinton Economic Boom

(and Other Myths of the Clinton Presidency)

By B. A. Marbue Brown

Acknowledgements

Special thanks to the Somerset County Library System of Somerset County, New Jersey, especially the branch located in Hillsborough. Also, special thanks to the King County Library system of King County, Washington, especially the branches located in Sammamish and Bellevue. Without the extensive online access to content from newspapers, magazines, journals and other sources that these public libraries make available to their patrons, this project would not have been possible. Moreover, the assistance provided by reference librarians, either in person or through an online service like "Ask a librarian," was instrumental in facilitating the research that forms the basis of this book.

Special thanks to my wife who put up with the impossible hours required to meet the challenges of a demanding job plus this project, which used up every spare moment left over.

Special thanks to family members and friends who read excerpts of the manuscript or its entirety and provided candid comments as well as editorial advice.

Table of Contents

∽:∾

Introduction

"If you tell the same story five times, it's true."

Larry Speakes
Reagan Press Secretary

You've probably heard it said that there are only two sure things in life: death and taxes. But, in an election year, just as sure as death and taxes, one can be sure that there will be charges and counter-charges, claims and counter-claims. Like it or not these are the building blocks of political campaigns. Candidates make claims about their own records and charges about the "other guy's" record. Candidates make claims about their own policies and charges about the "other guy's" policies. It's left to the electorate to evaluate the authenticity of these claims and charges. More often than not voters probably rely on gut feeling to decide who to believe, but usually there is objective evidence that voters can appeal to that will help them make up their minds. The problem is that this information is not necessarily easily accessible or available in a user friendly form leaving the electorate with little choice other than to go with the ad hoc approach.

The presidential campaigns of 2000 and 2004 were no different, and the campaigns for the foreseeable future won't be any different either. During the presidential campaigns of '00 and '04 many claims were made about the accomplishments of the Clinton administration, and those claims continued during the protracted campaign of 2008, which is still in progress as this is being written. Among other things candidates have claimed that the Clinton administration was responsible for the extraordinary economic boom of the '90s as well as the creation of 22 million jobs during that period. The Clinton administration also took credit for balancing the federal budget and welfare reform.

Interestingly enough the Democrats were largely unchallenged on these claims and now it is widely accepted that these claims are in fact true. But are they? Was Clinton's fiscal policy the catalyst for the economic boom or was Clinton simply in the right place at the right time? Was Clinton the champion of welfare reform or did he simply manage to insert some of his ideas into the final outcome of this debate while someone else led the way? It would be extremely useful to voters to have the answers to these questions because if Clinton policies were responsible for the boom of the '90s, this would provide a powerful argument in favor of electing leaders who would embrace these policies and give America a chance of returning to the prosperity of that truly extraordinary period. Alternately, if Clinton policies were not responsible for the 90's boom, the public would want to know who or what actually was responsible.

Against this backdrop, the author set out to explore the foundations of the conventional wisdom about some of the accomplishments that are most frequently attributed to the Clinton administration, including the booming '90s economy, 22 million newly created jobs, the balanced budget, and welfare reform. The findings were quite fascinating. It turns out that some widely held beliefs about what the administration achieved are based on myths. This could have some important implications for how the nation tackles its economic and related public policy challenges. As a result, this volume has been put together to share the background details that led to this conclusion. In its pages, three prevalent beliefs about the Clinton record are exposed as myths. Along the way a lot of helpful economic and public policy information is also revealed. What has emerged out of this project is a compilation of material that is thought provoking, educational and entertaining.

A disclaimer is in order here. This is not an exercise in Clinton bashing. Instead it is an attempt at an objective analysis of the relevant facts, allowing the chips to fall where they may. Because of the nature of the subject matter, the dialogue is bound to seem a bit political at times, but those who stick with it will find that that there is much more material about what works in terms of driving the economy or implementing public policy than there is about raw politics.

Chapter 1: Myth One - The Clinton Economic Boom

ᴄ᷎:᷎ᴗ

According to a press release from the Clinton White House on December 3, 1999, the economic expansion of the 1990s was due in large part to the President's three-part economic strategy of fiscal discipline, investing in the American people, and opening markets abroad[1]. It is only natural that a sitting president would take credit for positive phenomena that happened on his watch; however, the empirical evidence points elsewhere for the main drivers of the economic expansion of the '90s. In particular, empirical evidence suggests that five factors combined to create the extraordinary economic climate of the '90s:

- The Year 2K "bug"
- Creation of the World Wide Web and a user friendly interface to access it: The Browser
- The Telecom Act of 1996
- Cheap Money
- Large pool of unsophisticated investors

Any one of these by itself would have provided a potent economic stimulus. After all, the economic stimulus package proposed by Clinton himself when he first took the reins of state was on the order of $16.3 billion. Each of these factors poured many times more dollars than that into the economy. The combination of all five of them created the economic equivalent of the perfect storm, i.e., an enormous concentration of positive economic energy unlikely to be duplicated in the lifetime of those who witnessed it. Together they poured somewhere in the neighborhood of 13 trillion dollars into the economy during the Clinton years, most of it during the 5-year period from 1995 - 2000. They created jobs that paid much higher than average salaries and turned high-tech workers into the equivalent of rock stars and celebrities. Before this period when did anyone ever hear of programmers getting signing bonuses for accepting a job or retention bonuses for staying on for a specified period of time? Perhaps this was the case in pockets here and there but certainly not on a widespread basis. These types of perks were typically reserved for corporate executives, but in the latter half of the 90's they were commonplace among tech sector workers.

The economic "Fab Five" spawned shopping sprees of mammoth proportions in both the business-to-business and business-to-consumer sectors of the economy. And, these shopping sprees were for big ticket items in both sectors, networking equipment and wireless spectrum in the business-to-business sector, second homes and luxury cars in the business-to-consumer sector. These shopping sprees helped relatively young companies to mature quickly and become well-established, dependable market leaders.

The combination of these five economic drivers boosted tax revenues, inflated the value of retirement funds, and padded corporate earnings. Each positive outcome gave birth to another creating a huge self sustaining force field. Economists were at a loss to explain it. Fund managers were not sure how to respond to it. Politicians for the most part were surprised by it.

When "The Perfect Storm" hit the New England coast in October 1991, three weather systems each of which would have packed a powerful punch as a standalone came together to create a storm so powerful that some scientists said the formation of the storm, and its retrogression, made it a freak, a "hundred year storm."[2] In many respects, the same can be said about the economic environment of the '90s, i.e., just like a perfect storm is an extremely rare event, so we can expect that the economic boom of the '90s was an extremely rare event. The Y2K bug was a once in a thousand year phenomenon, if not more rare now that we understand what caused it. E-business strategists routinely referred to the Internet boom as a once in a hundred year event. The bottom line is that given that any one of these economic stimuli by itself is rare, one can expect that the combination of them in the same time frame is even rarer.

However, in every election since Bill Clinton exhausted his eligibility to run, one of the common campaign themes has been "Elect me and I'll return you to the prosperity of the '90s." In fact, some of Senator Hilary Clinton's popularity as a presidential candidate for 2008 could be attributed to the notion that she could bring back the prosperity of the Bill Clinton years.

Perhaps some measure of the '90s economic expansion can be recaptured, but the American public shouldn't be expecting something of the same order of magnitude. What's more, if the factors that created the expansion are not well understood, our leaders will be at a loss to recreate it. And, it is not clear that our leading politicians understand what happened here. Think back to Campaign 2000. Remember all of the discussion by candidates from both parties about what to do with the budget surplus that was projected 10 years out? The unstated assumption underlying this debate was that economic conditions would remain the same. No one acknowledged the possibility that they might change or that at some point over the planning period there might not be a surplus, much less that there might not be a surplus in the short run. The prevailing sentiment at the time was that a new day had dawned as far as the economy was concerned and that we had entered a period of virtually uninterrupted economic growth. None of the old rules applied anymore. But, conditions did change and the surplus disappeared with it.

The only conclusions that can be drawn from this is that either politicians did not have a good grasp of the economic forces at play or that they did and chose to ignore them for political reasons. Either way, promises of returning to Clinton era prosperity ring hollow and if the electorate buys into the hype, chances are they will wind up being short changed.

It is important to make a careful study of how we achieved such an extraordinary period of growth and to tease out the key drivers so that we can apply them deliberately to public policy. We may not achieve perfect storm conditions for some time to come, but at least we can give ourselves the best chance to keep the economy moving in the right direction. In this section of the book we think we've done just that. After a careful analysis of the evidence, we believe that an economic perfect storm driven by the five factors identified earlier is the best explanation for the Booming '90s, not Clinton administration policy. Over the course of the next several chapters, we'll discuss each of the drivers and then outline the lessons learned from them. We invite you to follow along and see what you conclude after you review the evidence.

Chapter 2: The Year 2K "bug"

"Unless they are fixed . . . All computer programs .
. . Everywhere in the world . . . Will go on strike on
January 1st 2000 . . . Can you imagine . . . just for a
moment . . . the chaos this would cause? There would
be no air traffic, no traffic lights, no lights in your
company, companies could not produce goods, no
goods delivered to the stores, stores could not send
you bills, you could not send bills to anyone else.
Business would come to a halt."[3]

> Peter de Jager
> January, 1997

In the 1990's a new phrase was introduced into the American vocabulary: "Y2K bug" (also known as the Millennium bug, Year 2000 problem, and a variety of other names). This phrase referred to the longstanding practice of using two digits to store the year portion of dates in computer programs, which in turn could cause computers to misinterpret dates and malfunction at the dawn of the new millennium. Until then most people probably had not given much thought to that fact that midnight on December 31, 1999 would signal the beginning of a new millennium and that with it might come some major disruptions in our way of life. Some may have given thought to bigger, more extravagant New Year's celebrations, perhaps even special mementos of the new millennium but figured after that it would be business as usual. No such luck!!!

Most readers are probably well aware of at least some of the threats posed by computer malfunctions, but just in case you aren't, let's review. Among other things the Y2K bug threatened to shut off power, telephones, water and other utilities. It threatened to disrupt transportation systems, banking transactions and food supplies. There were even concerns about an accidental launch of nuclear weapons.

The Y2K bug originated with a programming decision in the '60s motivated by a need to save space at a time when computer storage was relatively expensive; yet it became one of the most powerful economic forces of the 1990's. Why? It's because by the mid 1990's, computers had invaded nearly every aspect of American life including business, the marketplace, the home and even leisure. By the mid-1990's about 85 million PCs were in use in the United States[4] and every major business process was computerized, including payroll, inventory, invoicing and so on. In the realm of everyday living computerized items included banking, check out registers at stores, gas pumps, traffic lights, automobile diagnostics, airplane navigation, and even household appliances like microwave ovens.

Year	Cost of a megabyte of RAM (Random Access Memory)
1970	$3,200,000
1980	$64,000
1990	$120
1995	$30
1997	$5
1998	$1
Source: CNN.com	

No one could take the chance that our way of life would come to halt as the clock struck midnight on December 31, 1999, especially considering that reports of Y2K related hiccups had already begun to surface years in advance of D-day. For example, credit cards with expiration dates in 2000 were being erroneously rejected at checkout counters because computers thought they had expired 98 years ago. Some homeowners were receiving mortgage bills with errors because computer programs were having trouble with interest calculations for mortgages maturing in the year 2000. Handwriting was on the wall that without attention to this matter, the ramifications could be quite serious. Only there was one little catch: the fix for the Y2K bug was not trivial nor was it inexpensive. In fact, it was downright labor intensive. This of course had its good points and its bad points. On the one hand, businesses found themselves in the undesirable position of being in a race with the clock and needing to shell out a lot of cash to avoid major setbacks. On the other hand, this state of affairs created enormous opportunities for those who had the skills, intellectual property and other assets that could be used to remediate the Y2K problem. IT professionals whose skills had once been declared obsolete suddenly found themselves in great demand. What's more, the urgency of problem made it possible for these folks to command premium salaries. Thus, was born a multi-billion dollar industry with a limited, compressed lifespan.

Y2K Economic Stimulus Beats Clinton Economic Stimulus

Estimates of the cost of remediating the Y2K bug range from $100-$200 billion[5] in the U.S. to as much as $600 billion[6] worldwide. Either way this amounts to a significant economic stimulus. It dwarfs any economic stimulus package proposed by the Clinton administration or the George W.

Bush (Bush 43) administration. Much of this went directly toward the salaries of Information Technology workers who managed or executed Y2K remediation projects. These salaries in turn were inflated by the shortage of available resources and the compressed time frame in which the task had to be accomplished. Below are the average salaries paid by the top 10 consulting firms for various Y2K assignments as reported in the June 29, 1998 issue of Business Week:[7]

Title	Base Salary	Bonus	Incentives
Project Director	$110,000	13%	Long-term incentives
Project Manager	$87,900	16%	Long-term incentives
Senior Programmer	$70,300	5%	Long-term incentives
Quality Assurance Analyst	$53,100	-	Short-term incentives

Most Americans would agree that these are pretty good salaries, and the top 10 consulting firms weren't the only ones paying them. Other sources (Senior Staff 2000[8], Volt Services Group[9], Wawa[10]) quoting salaries for Y2K programmers in hourly terms reported figures ranging from $35 an hour at the low end to as much as $150 an hour at the high end[11]. The low-end figure of $35 an hour translates to $67,000 annually assuming full-time employment with four weeks off for vacation and holidays. Some freelancers reported annual salaries in excess of $110,000[12].

The urgency of the Y2K problem also caused employers to provide all kinds of incentives to get candidates to sign on or to keep existing employees from defecting to another more lucrative offer. For example, in January 1999, Computerworld reported that COBOL programmers in San Diego were receiving quarterly bonuses of $1000 to $1200 on $50,000 - $60,000 salaries plus bonuses of $6000 to $9000 for completing their Y2K projects[13]. These are somewhat less than what had been predicted at one point but still pretty good extra money by most people's standards. Perhaps an even more telling example is the following quote from a director of information services at a major financial services company in New York reported in the February 1, 1999 issue of InfoWorld[14]:

> "We gave a $30,000 bonus for those who agreed to stay on until 2000. But you know what? Good people still left anyway for the reason that the bonuses [couldn't match] the signing bonuses that firms were giving to experienced COBOL programmers."

What's more, Y2K-related incentives were not limited to hiring and retention but also extended to "combat" pay for workers who needed to be kept on to support contingency plans during the '99-'00 New Year's holiday weekend. One company Burson - Marsteller rewarded employees with a $2000 bonus, a free hotel getaway and a bottle of champagne. They were not alone. A survey by consulting firm William M. Mercer showed that about 16% of companies rewarded employees with additional pay while 56% offered employees additional paid time off[15].

Even the federal government was forced to hike salaries and get creative with incentives. A 1998 GAO report ("Year 2000 Computing Crisis: Status of Efforts to Deal with Personnel Issues" [GGD-99-14]) cited delays at several agencies due to inability to hire qualified staff. It also cited one agency that had lost 28 technology workers in the first six months of fiscal 1998. Though not specifically stated, this was likely due to more lucrative offers from employers in the private sector competing for the same resources. As a result, federal agencies were authorized to offer lump sum payments of up to 25 percent of basic pay to a new employee or to an employee who needed to relocate. Agencies were also allowed to pay out retention bonuses of up to 25 percent of basic pay and give performance awards of up to $10,000. Agencies were given the option to waive the reduction of pensions for re-employed retired military officers as well as the reduction of pay for civilian annuitants who needed to be rehired to perform Y2K repairs.

To put these salaries and incentives in perspective, one has to take into account that the already tight market for IT professionals became much tighter during the mid-90's as Y2K remediation efforts and the Internet boom peaked at roughly the same time. In 1999, in the midst of Y2K reme-diation efforts Meta Group, a Stamford, Conn. research firm, estimated that 400,000 IT jobs would go unfilled while Information Technology Association of America estimated a shortage of 346,000 workers and the Computer Technology Industry Association predicted a shortage 269,000[16]. There is a fair amount of variation in these estimates, but it's pretty clear that the experts agreed that the available talent was not commensurate with the tasks at hand, Y2K remedia-tion being one of them. The competition for these resources created an IT job seekers' market and drove new recruitment and retention paradigms, which in turn hiked compensation for IT professionals overall and put extra cash their pockets. Armed with extra disposable cash, these folks poured this money back into the economy in the form of big ticket purchases and securities investments.

Fixing the Millennium Bug Translates to Phenomenal Job Growth

Estimates of exactly how many jobs were created by the need to solve the Y2K bug are in short supply. However, it is pretty clear that number was quite substantial. In 1997, world renowned Y2K experts like Howard Rubin made forward looking projections about how many programmers would be needed to address the Millennium bug based on the amount of code that had to be repaired. These projections put the number of programmers needed at 500,000 to 700,000 in addition to those who were already hard at work on the Y2K problem[17]. However, there isn't any mention of the number of resources that were already in service. Other references to the number of Y2K workers are found in the context of estimates that surfaced as prognosticators made predictions about what would happen to the Y2K workforce once the crisis was over. These references can be found in trade magazines like Information Week (August 17, 1998)[18] as well as popular press like USA Today (January 3, 2000)[19], and they put the number of Y2K workers in the 500,000 range.

The number of jobs created by Y2K could also be estimated based on how much money was spent on Y2K remediation and what proportion of those funds were allocated to staff costs. In November 1998 Cap Gemini released the results of a Y2K study that examined the progress of remediation efforts in 12 countries as well as the associated costs. Among other things, the study found that in between April and November of 1998, $238 billion was spent globally on fixing the Y2K bug. In addition the study found that during that period, one fifth of these funds was spent on hardware, one fifth was spent on software, and the remaining three fifths (60%) was spent on staff costs[20]. The funds allocation from the Cap Gemini study provides a good benchmark of how

Y2K money was spent, and it can be used to develop a credible estimate of how many jobs in the US were supported by Y2K initiatives.

First, recall that $100 billion to $200 billion was spent in the US on Y2K fixes. Next, figure how much of this was allocated to staff costs by taking 60% of the total, which puts the figure for staff costs at $60 billion to $120 billion. The next step is to divide the staff costs by the average cost of a Y2K worker. Even if the average staff costs worked out to be as high as $200,000 for salary plus other related costs, this would translate to 300,000 to 600,000 jobs. However, from salary information provided earlier, it's clear that the average cost of a Y2K worker is much less than this.

The Economic Curse that Became Blessing

Another angle on the economic prosperity ignited by the Millennium bug is the boost in revenue and profits it provided to start-ups, fledgling, and established companies alike, including systems integrators, boutique consultancies, and tools vendors. Keane Inc., a midsized IT services firm, is an excellent illustration of a company that enjoyed significantly improved financials as a result of the stimulus provided by the Y2K bug. In September of 1997 Keane announced that it would increase its workforce by 45%, hiring 4000 workers most of whom would be focused on Y2K projects. In 1996 just 1 percent of the company's revenue was derived from Y2K related projects. However, in 1997 Keane took in around $125 million in Y2K related revenue or about 20% of its total[21]. The Y2K windfall continued in 1998 when in the first quarter alone, Keane took in $71 million in revenue from Y2K projects, and by mid-1998 Keane's Y2K revenues constituted about 34% of its total. As might be expected, Keane's stock performance also benefited from its Y2K business, increasing by 71% between December of 1997 and June of 1998[22].

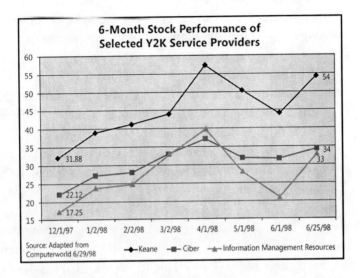

Another example of a company that benefited from a boost in revenue and profits due to Y2K is Peritus Software Services. Y2K business helped Peritus grow from an $18 million business in 1995 to a $40 million business in 1998 with a market capitalization of nearly $200 million[23]. The company's revenue doubled in one year on the strength of its Y2K solution. When it first offered its stock for sale to the public, the offer price was set at $16, but the stock actually opened at $25.50[24]. Viasoft, a company with a similar solution to Peritus, saw its stock price increase by eightfold in 1996 on the buzz created by its Y2K offerings[25].

The stories of Keane, Peritus, and Viasoft were repeated many times over. Below are some additional examples:

- In 1997, at Computer Associates International, Y2K-related product lines grew 800 percent over a six-month period[26]

- Information Week reported that Amdahl's Y2K revenues reached $100 million in 1997 and had the potential to double in 1998[27].
- Computer Horizons revenue for second quarter 1997 was 35% higher than the corresponding quarter for 1996 and net income was 127% higher on the strength of the company's Y2K business[28]
- According to the Global IT Consulting Report, the top 50 IT consulting firms grew at a rate of 27% in 1997 largely due to the need for Y2K fixes[29].
- In 1999 alone, Ernst & Young projected 33% growth and unveiled plans to add an additional 1000 workers

Not only did the Y2K bug create jobs in the Information Technology sector, but it also gave birth to a whole new emergency preparedness movement, which drove sales of gas powered electric generators, bottled water, canned foods, lanterns, flashlights, storage containers of various types, ready-to-eat meals, portable toilets, and a variety of other survival supplies. Comprehensive estimates of the extent of the impact of this movement are hard to come by. However, a few data points are worth taking into account. First, Y2K sales had a significant impact on the financials of the world's largest home improvement retailer: the Home Depot. In fact, the impact was so significant that Home Depot mentioned it as a key driver of the outstanding year-over-year improvement in its sales from 3rd quarter of 1998 to 3rd quarter of 1999. Meanwhile, the Home Depot also referred to the Y2K impact as the main driver of the unfavorable comparison of 3rd quarter 2000 financials versus those of 3rd quarter 1999[30]. Other reports indicate that the precipitous drop in sales was one of the factors that contributed to Home Depot's replacement of its CEO.

A second data point is Sunbeam Corp., a conglomerate that distributes, among other things, Powermate generators, camp stoves and lanterns. According to the Sun Sentinel (Fort Lauderdale, Fl.), losses at Sunbeam in the second quarter of 2000 worsened by 70 percent over the same period of the previous year, as the company blamed a Y2K-related sales drop off. The following quote from Sunbeam's CEO Jerry W. Levin leaves no ambiguity about Sunbeam management's perspective on the impact of Y2K on their business[31].

"We underestimated the degree to which the sale of Y2K related products... impacted our results in 1999 and would cannibalize 2000 sales in these categories"

A third data point is concerned with the third quarter 2000 financial results for Duracell and Energizer, two of the Big 3 battery producers. Duracell's sales were down 9 percent for third quarter 2000 and profits were down by 26 percent compared with third quarter 1999. Statements by Eveready CEO J. Patrick Mulcahy indicate the same type of pattern at his company[32]:

"For the important October through December battery selling season, we expect a very difficult comparison due to last year's Y2K demand."
"Last year, alkaline category sales were up 28 percent vs. historical increases in the 7 percent range. As consumer takeaway returns to normal historical trends, we anticipate that the category will experience a decline, compared with the exceptional growth in the last three months of 1999"

In addition to the empirical evidence from these major firms, anecdotal evidence from smaller military surplus, outdoor recreation, and hardware stores give evidence of a Y2K-related boost in sales. For example, in an interview with the Los Angeles Times, Peter and Gary Kalaydjian, owners of Recon-1 in Tarzana, CA indicated that most gear and supplies were selling at four to five times the usual pace in December 1999. One popular Y2K item, 55-gallon water drums, were selling at a rate of 100 per week compared with the normal rate of 100 per year[33]. In an article published in National Home Center News in February 1999[34], Carol Watkins, owner of Oceanway Hardware in Jacksonville, Florida is quoted as saying "We used to sell one pitcher pump every three weeks or so. Now we can't keep them in stock. We've increased our order about 300 percent, and it's still not enough." It turns out that after inquiring about customers' reasons for purchasing the pumps, Carol found that the purchase was Y2K-related. Also in the National Home Center News article, the owner of Clark Do-it-Center in Ellicott City, MD reported that her store has quadrupled its purchases of generators and kerosene heaters while owners of a Mennonite store based in Kidron Ohio indicated that they had added people to their order processing and shipping departments with many working overtime. Similar evidence is found in an article published in Marketing News in May 1999 where Bill Poynot, owner of Perret's Army and Navy Stores in New Orleans indicated his sales were up 20% to 25% from the previous year[35]. The anecdotal evidence covers the East Coast, West Coast, and the middle of the country as well as the beginning, middle and end of 1999. They all indicate the same pattern, i.e., substantially increased sales activity due to Y2K preparations.

The exact extent of the economic impact of the Y2K bug is hard to quantify, but the evidence that has been provided so far shows that the economic impact of the Y2K was enormous and pervasive. The Y2K bug created a boat load of jobs, energized a variety of industries (e.g., IT services, emergency/survival supplies, recruitment and staffing), gave birth to oodles of new companies, put loads of extra money in people's pockets or in other words elevated disposable income, and triggered a wave of discretionary spending.

Using the $200 billion price tag for Y2K remediation in the US, this translates of an economic stimulus package of about $40 billion a year for five years. However, it's clear that the dollars funneled into the economy were much, much more than what was devoted to remediation efforts. The irony of the Y2K bug is that it was anticipated to be an economic curse; instead it turned out to be an economic blessing.

The Clinton Administration: Missing in Action on Solving Y2K

Practically all of the money spent on Y2K remediation was spent between 1995 and 2000, i.e., right in the middle of the Clinton years. Many of the high wage jobs that the Clinton administration takes credit for were related to Y2K either directly or indirectly. So what was the Clinton administration's role in the Y2K remediation effort? Did it lead the way in educating the public about the problem or identifying strategies for solving it? Did the administration create a master plan to drive the country toward Y2K readiness? Did the administration create regulation or national policy of any kind that would be a catalyst for Y2K preparations? Any of these would be a legitimate basis on which the Clinton administration could claim that it was somehow responsible for some of the economic benefit that accrued to the country as a result of the Y2K bug. Just to clarify, this is not about whether the administration did anything at all and it is certainly not about whether the administration viewed Y2K as an economic opportunity. However, it is about whether the administration recognized a national emergency early on, provided leadership to guide the country through it, and reaped economic stimulus as a byproduct.

All indications are that the Clinton administration was a laggard when it came to Y2K preparations. It wasn't until 1998 that the president appointed a Y2K Czar. The president himself did not address the Y2K problem publicly until July 1998[36]. By this time the problem was well known within the business community and remediation was well underway. In fact, in mid-1998, Big 6 consulting firms put the word out that they would stop accepting new Y2K business[37]. Around the same time, Keane, the consulting firm who boasted that it had completed more Y2K remediation projects than any other consultant, stopped offering their sales force bonuses for signing Y2K new business.

Peter De Jager is credited with getting the ball rolling for Y2K remediation with his "Doomsday" article published in Computerworld magazine in 1993[38]. Next, the Big 6 (now the Final Four) accounting firms picked up the mantra and alerted their audit customers to the problem and the need to address it. Shortly thereafter, these companies began offering their clients Y2K remediation services. For example, Cap Gemini America started its Y2K practice in 1994, and by late 1997 they had signed up nearly 200 customers for Y2K remediation projects[39]. By mid-1997, Keane Inc., one of the leading firms in the Y2K remediation business, had sold a cumulative total of 291 Y2K remediation engagements with an estimated value of $340 million[40].

The Information Week 500 presents Information Week's analysis and ranking of the most innovative corporate users of information technology. Companies selected for the 1997 class of the Information Week 500 indicated on average that 52% of their code was Y2K compliant with some industries like Insurance indicating compliance rates as high as 63%[41]. Gillette, one of the companies interviewed for the Information Week 500, indicated that about 80% of its code was Y2K compliant and that it had begun a Y2K awareness campaign 18 months prior that included a detailed assessment of what needed to be fixed and how much it would cost[42]. In March 1998, a survey conducted by Howard Rubin, a highly regarded expert Y2K expert, found that a full-fledged Y2K strategy was already underway in 60% companies that responded[43]. A follow-up survey in June of 1998 showed that 86% of companies had a full fledged Y2K strategy in place, all this before President Clinton ever addressed the issue publicly.

Leadership in the federal government on the Y2K issue primarily came from Congress. Representatives Steve Horn (R-Calif), Tom Davis (R.-VA), and Constance Morella (R-MD) began holding hearings on the Y2K problem in April of 1996 and kept tabs on the progress of government agencies throughout the process[44]. Representative Horn, chairman of the House subcommittee on technology, drew public attention to the Y2K issue and set the tone for the Federal government's Y2K remediation efforts by handing out report cards, which graded federal agencies on their Y2K readiness. The first round of grades was handed out in July of 1996, and as one might expect, they were not good. In fact, up to mid-1998 the overall administration still received an "F" from Representative Horn's grading system[45]. Administration officials were not happy with the grades they received and sometimes disputed them. Nevertheless, the reports cards had the desired effect as officials' embarrassment over lousy grades became a catalyst to accelerate Y2K initiatives in many federal agencies.

In addition to the report card initiative, Rep. Horn was very vocal on the Y2K issue repeatedly calling on the President to get involved in familiarizing the public with the subject. For example in mid-1998 Rep. Horn was quoted in USA Today as follows[46]:

"We urge (President Clinton) again to use the bully pulpit. Not to create public panic, but to explain the nature of the issue"

Similarly, in a letter to the White House Office of Management and Budget (OMB) in December of 1997, Rep. Horn, called on the Executive branch to step up its efforts on Y2K conversion and specifically called on the President or OMB Director Raines to appoint a "full time" coordinator to "spearhead the Y2K correction effort." Below is an excerpt from the letter published in Defense Daily on December 12, 1997[47]:

"It is time to pick up the pace and raise the standards. We have concentrated, and properly so, on "mission critical" systems. Now we must expand our scope to include the next tier of systems. We have accepted misleading reports, sloppy and incoherent data, and overly optimistic schedules. Now, with the chief information officers in place, OMB needs to require agency plans and reports that are more comprehensive and reliable."

But for the efforts by Congress, the Federal government might not have completed its remediation efforts on time. Early on when the private sector was ramping up to tackle the problem, Y2K was barely on the Federal government's radar. This is vividly illustrated by the difference between Y2K revenue of federal integrators versus their private sector counterparts in the 1997 time frame. While private sector integrators were reporting tens of millions in quarterly revenue and double digit growth due to Y2K business, CACI, an Arlington, VA-based federal integrator, reported that only about $1 million of its $70 million was due to Y2K business. Other federal integrators observed the same dearth of spending by federal agencies in 1997[48]:

"For the most part, nobody's spending enough on it yet that people can say they're really making money."

Jack Littley
Sr. VP & Director Corporate Development
BTG

There's also plenty of other evidence that instead of taking the lead in addressing the Y2K problem Federal agencies were playing catch up. For example, in April of 1997, Computer Reseller News reported that Joel Willemson, Director of Resources Information Management for the General Accounting Office, had told Congress that because agencies had not planned well enough to get all the reprogramming done in time, "there is a high probability there will be some failures."[49] Along the same lines, comments by federal officials reported in the August 3, 1998 edition of the Washington Post[50] revealed that in 1996 one federal agency had bought a security system that would fail to recognize employee passes after the turn of the century, and as late as 1997, some agencies were still writing new code that would not work after midnight on December 31, 1999.

Because the government got started so late on its own remediation efforts, even after the president's council was in place, much of its attention was focused on ensuring that federal agencies would be ready on time let alone providing leadership for industry at large. The bottom line is that despite the fact that Vice President Gore was considered to be a champion of technology issues, the Clinton Administration was not on top of this issue. Initially, the administration may have regarded calls for Y2K readiness by the Republican led Congress as an attempt to find an issue where there wasn't really one. What ever the reason, the administration did not get involved until quite late in the game. As a result, it can't take credit for the economic by-product of Y2K remediation initiatives. The Clinton administration certainly helped to solve the Y2K problem but it did not lead. Consequently, it can't take credit for the economic windfall.

Chapter 3: Creation of the World Wide Web and a User Friendly Interface to Access It: The Browser

"When I took office, only high energy physicists had ever heard of what is called the Worldwide Web — when I took office, January of 1993, only high energy physicists had heard of it. Now even my cat has its own Web page."[51]

Bill Clinton
Knoxville, TN
October, 1996

The influence of the Internet is so pervasive today that we forget that at the beginning of the '90s, the average American had no clue what the Internet was. Words and phrases like browser, chat room, email, e-commerce, IM, and pop-ups were not a part of the everyday vernacular. In fact, even now many people are not aware of the subtle distinction between the Internet and the World Wide Web as we tend to use these two labels interchangeably.

Today we check email even when we are on vacation. One hardly checks into a hotel without finding out what types of Internet connections are available. We bank online, book travel online, buy Christmas presents online, check weather online, file income tax returns online, renew automobile registrations online, search for jobs online, take courses online, and the list goes on. At one point, the combined trading accomplished on just one website, Ebay, the leading online auction website, was larger than the gross domestic product of all but 70 of the world's countries[52]. During the '07 holiday shopping season, consumers spent $29.2 billion online[53]. Experts are estimating that in '08 the volume of goods and services bought and sold on the Internet will be around $200 billion.

Clearly, the Internet has had a significant impact on the US and world economy. The period during which the Internet gained widespread adoption and experienced the most growth coincided with the Clinton administration, i.e., 1994 -2001. So what was the Clinton Administration's role in all this? Did it somehow have a part in launching this revolution or did it play a major role in sustaining it? If so, the administration could legitimately take credit for some of the economic benefit that accrued to the country as a result of the Internet revolution. On the other the hand, if the Internet revolution occurred largely without any leadership or vital contributions from the administration, then credit ought to be given where credit is due. More importantly, the public needs to understand the real economic lessons of this phenomenon so that it will be easier to recognize the next landmark opportunity and so that we can be smarter about how to manage it as well as benefit from it. It is also important for the public to understand these lessons so that they can be on their guard against false hopes raised by politicians during campaign season.

Two factors had a major impact on the Internet's rise to prominence in the American way of life, and the Clinton administration had very little to do with either. The first of these two factors is the invention of the World Wide Web (www). The Internet had already been around for quite a while by the time the World Wide Web was created in 1991. Over 700,000 computers were already connected and over 4,000,000 people used it, but it was mostly used in the scientific, commercial R&D, and military communities[54]. The World Wide Web helped to change all that by creating a hypertext based system that allowed users to jump from one document to another even if the latter document was on a completely different Internet host. We take this type of hypertext linking for granted today, but prior to the release of the World Wide Web, exchanging information between computers on the Internet was much more involved and as a result uninteresting to the general public.

Interestingly enough, the World Wide Web was invented at a research laboratory in Switzerland to improve accessibility of information for researchers After its release in 1991 by Tim Berners Lee, it was quickly recognized that the potential of the World Wide Web extended far beyond applications in scientific research. It wasn't the product of an R&D project to develop a killer application. There was no grand vision to change the world. It was simply the outcome of a research scientist trying to find a better way to do his job. Yet, it had a tremendous impact on the economic prosperity of the '90s.

The second key factor that helped catapult the Internet to prominence was the development of browsers, which provided a user friendly interface to the Web and introduced the possibility of mixing text and graphics. The most notable of these were MOSAIC, Netscape Navigator, and Microsoft's Internet Explorer. These browsers overcame a number of obstacles that had hindered widespread adoption of the Internet, e.g., intuitive navigation, retrieval of general interest documents. MOSAIC was developed by Marc Andreesen and Eric Bina at the National Center for Supercomputing Applications (NCSA) at the University of Illinois and made available to the general public in 1993. Within weeks of its posting, MOSAIC had been downloaded by tens of thousands of users and its popularity with the end-user community was unmistakable. MOSAIC's popularity was picked up by the mainstream media and as a result the Internet, a medium whose familiarity was limited to those who had a need to know, became known to the general public.

The one thing that is conspicuously absent from this discussion of the drivers of the Internet revolution is the role of the Clinton administration in all of this. Sure the government provided funding for NCSA, but to be sure the creation of MOSAIC was not high on the list of priorities for the technology incubator. It's not like funding was provided with the creation of an Internet revolution in mind. At most the creation of MOSAIC was a blip on the administration's radar screen, at least until it gained the attention of the public at large. Instead this revolution appears to be an example of free enterprise at its best. It has all of the ingredients: self-started inventors, private investors, and minimal intervention from the government

The combination of the invention of the World Wide Web and browsers resulted in explosive growth in Internet usage. At the end of 1991 there were about 4,000,000 users. By the end of 1998, four years after the release of Netscape Navigator, the browser which first made the Internet accessible to the general public, there were 147 million users[55]. Explosive growth in turn led to identification of new applications for the Internet, which in turn led to more users and the cycle continued. By the end of 2000 there were 361 million users worldwide[56]. With these kinds of numbers, the size of Internet audiences rivaled those of traditional media outlets with the added benefit that it practically eliminated geographical boundaries. As business leaders and investors recognized the potential of this new medium for advertising, business process automation, and globalization, the economic fireworks really began.

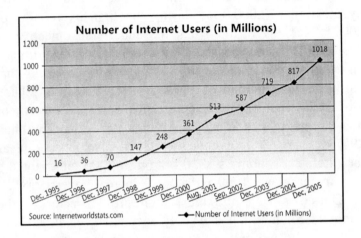

The Browser Gives Birth to a Whole New Economy: The Internet Economy

The success of the Internet created so much economic activity that it reached the level of being tracked as a full-blown economy in its own right, which was dubbed the Internet economy. The Internet economy was practically non-existent at the beginning of the 1990s, but by the end of the decade it was sporting spectacular statistics. According to a study commissioned by Cisco Systems and published by the University of Texas Center for Research in Electronic Commerce, in 2000 the Internet economy supported about 3.1 million jobs and was producing about $830 billion in revenue[57]. At the time, that represented more jobs than the insurance industry, the real estate industry, and even the federal government. This is pretty impressive for a phenomenon that wasn't on anybody's radar only a few years before.

As businesses rushed to participate in the Internet economy, the growth statistics were equally as spectacular. According to the Cisco/UT report, the Internet economy created around 650,000 jobs in 1999 but topped that easily by creating 612,000 jobs during the first six months of 2000[58]. Keeping in mind that the underlying objective of this book is to consider the Clinton administration's impact on the economic boom of the 1990's, it's worth noting that during the first quarter of 2000, growth of internet related jobs at Internet economy companies outpaced growth of non-Internet related jobs by a factor of better than four, i.e., 29% versus 6.9%[59]. Revenue growth was also outstanding as the Internet Economy's $830 billion in 2000 represented a 58% increase over 1999 and a 156% increase over 1998[60].

Dot-coms were the most high profile sector of the Internet economy, but they only accounted for about 12% of these jobs and only a little more than a quarter of them were information technology jobs[61]. By 2000 every major business had a website at least for marketing purposes, but many others were using their websites to conduct trade as well as for customer service applications. As a result, the Internet economy created jobs in a variety of other functions. In fact, the Internet economy created more jobs in sales and marketing than in any other category.

The Internet Economy Drives Salaries through the Roof

Like Y2K, the jobs created by the Internet economy tended to be at the upper end of the pay scale. For example, in a salary survey released by Internet World magazine in July 2001, salary information is provided for 16 web-related jobs, including Administration, Operations, Design, Content,

Development, and Marketing. In all but two cases the median salary for these jobs was in excess of $50,000 annually, and for more than half of the job categories the median salary was in excess of $70,000 annually. The numbers look even better for those job holders who were eligible for incentives. Taking incentives into account, seven of the sixteen job categories had median total cash compensation in excess of $80,000 annually[62].

Another survey published by InfoWorld in June of 2000 gives additional evidence that the Internet economy produced jobs of the more lucrative variety. The InfoWorld survey compared compensation of IT professionals at Internet companies with their counterparts at non-Internet companies in a variety of areas, and the results are dramatic. For example, at Internet companies, 18% of respondents earned $100,000 or more in base salary. That is nearly twice the percentage of respondents at non-Internet companies who earned $100,000 or more. Similarly, at Internet companies nearly 22% received bonuses of $10,000 or more versus around 13% for non Internet companies. Again at Internet companies, around 23% of respondents had received a salary increase of greater than 20% of their base salary in the previous year as compared with just 10% for respondents from non-Internet companies[63].

In fact, Internet economy jobs, and particularly Dot-com jobs, had the effect of raising salaries for a wide variety of jobs. In addition to cash compensation, many Dot-com employees were also rewarded with stock options and they were often granted options before stock was offered to the public. This is important because the popularity of Internet stocks during that period once they hit the market made many Dot-com employees millionaires and even a few of them billionaires practically overnight. As a result, Dot-coms became a very appealing option to star performers and ambitious incumbents at traditional companies. A rash of defections forced traditional companies to respond with a variety of incentives to stem the tide of valuable employees leaving for the greener pastures of the Dot-com world.

The battle for the best and brightest during this period was nothing short of amazing. One of the more outrageous examples of this can be found in the April 16, 2000 issue of the Boston Globe, which described a full-page ad placed by Trilogy Software in a student newspaper near Cornell University's campus. The Trilogy ad promised the top five seniors with technical degrees an annual base salary of $200,000, plus benefits and a 2000 BMW 323 Ci coupe[64]. A similar example of excess is found in a Los Angeles Times article published May 23, 2000, which tells of a Pasadena-based company, ArsDigita, that rewarded employees with a free Ferrari for attracting ten programmers to the company[65]. In July of 1999 Information Week related the account of a New Jersey firm, Arcnet, whose CEO gave 28 employees newly leased BMWs with insurance included, 20 of which went to technology professionals[66]. There is no shortage of such accounts: Dot-coms taking their entire company to vacation in Hawaii, hiring full-time concierges to handle dry cleaning and other chores for time-pressed employees, Friday afternoon parties with game rooms and Foosball tables, and so on[67].

In February of 2000, the New York Times reported that over a two week period some of the nation's top law firms had raised pay for associates by as much as 50 percent, this in response to dozens of defections from law firms to Dot-com start-ups in Silicon Valley. These increases would enable first-year associates to earn more than $150,000 annually whereas during 1999 first-year associates' earnings were more in the neighborhood $100,000[68]. Of course, it wasn't just first-year associates who got pay raises. In this move some of the nation's top law firms added as much as $50 million to their individual payrolls[69].

The management consulting industry was also affected by competition from the Dot-coms as is indicated by the following quotes, which appeared in the May 9, 2000 issue of the Chicago Tribune

"The consulting companies are absolutely under attack from the Internet industry. They have a huge problem holding on to their associates"

Karl Aavik
Egon Zehnder

"We're running into Dot-coms all over the place. It's much more difficult to recruit talent because the lure of becoming a millionaire on paper is quite strong"

David Reed
Andersen Consulting
Director of U.S. Recruiting

In response, Accenture (previously Andersen Consulting) increased base compensation by 8% and announced that it would invest $200 million in e-commerce ventures with the returns redistributed to employees. This type of two-pronged response was typical across the industry with salaries being bumped as much as 10% and seed money being put up for e-commerce ventures to provide valuable employees with opportunities to get involved in the Internet economy[70].

In addition to the ones already mentioned, examples of the Dot-com effect can be cited from several other industries.

Accounting
Between 1992 and 1998, the number of people taking the exam to become certified public accountants dropped by 40 percent, and the American Institute of Certified Public

Accountants estimated that this was partially due to the impact of the Internet. At Arthur Andersen, then one of the top accounting firms in the country, salaries were bumped up by 10% in one year with some employees receiving raises of as much as a 30 percent[71].

Advertising

In the December 6, 1999 issue, Advertising Age tackled the impact of Dot-coms on salaries in the advertising industry by recounting the story of a media planner who with less than a year's experience went from a salary of $28,000 to $65,000 as a result of a bidding war. What's more this was not an isolated example. A human resources executive from a New York ad agency indicated that within a year of coming in at a salary of $30,000 junior account associates were commanding salaries of $45,000 to $50,000[72]. What were the drivers of these dramatic increases? To be sure, one of the key drivers was pressure from Dot-coms bidding for the same resources.

Banking

A survey of 300 bankers below the level of chief operating officer done by PricewaterhouseCoopers and published in late 1999, found that 60% were looking for new jobs[73]. Three main factors were mentioned as reasons for this phenomenon, and as you might have guessed, one of them was the opportunity to make a fortune by joining a Dot-com start-up or technology firm. The PricewaterhouseCoopers findings are corroborated by anecdotal information found in an article published in American Banker in early 2000 that dealt with defections from banking to Dot-coms. The article cited a New York recruitment executive who knew of 15 senior bankers that had left top companies to join Internet companies within a six-month period[74]. It almost goes without saying that one key aspect of the banking industry's response to Dot-com defections was increased compensation.

The bottom line is that Internet economy created a substantial number of high paying jobs and simultaneously boosted compensation in other sectors of the American economy. Dramatic increases were triggered by the basic laws of supply and demand as well as the old fashioned principle of "paying what the market will bear." Translation? It is true that the Clinton years were characterized by jobs and wage growth, but Clinton administration policy did not have a primary role in creating these Internet economy jobs or facilitating the upward movement in salaries that resulted from them.

The Internet Economy Breathes New Life into the Old Economy

The economic expansion driven by the Internet economy contributed to other types of jobs growth. In April of 2000, the Record of Stockton of California reported that a nonpartisan policy group found that two lower-end jobs were created in California for every lucrative high-tech position[75]. The report focused on some of the negative consequences of the growth of low-end jobs in high cost of living areas. Nevertheless, it also shed light on the impact of the Internet economy outside of its primary sphere of influence. If the California ratios held consistently throughout the country, somewhere in the neighborhood of 9 million jobs could be attributed to the impact of the Internet boom, i.e., 3.1 million Internet economy jobs and 6 million old economy jobs.

This notion of an employment multiplier effect is critical to understanding the job creation driven by the Internet economy, Y2K and the other nineties economic catalysts. For a long time economists have recognized that creation of jobs in "anchor" industries has a multiplier effect on other jobs in the economy in much the same way anchor stores in a mall generate other jobs by drawing the traffic that makes it profitable for other stores and establishments to locate there. In the US traditionally those anchor jobs have been in manufacturing and any significant expansion of jobs in the manufacturing sector would result in the creation of jobs in other segments of the economy.

For example, establishment of an auto plant creates new jobs in the plant but also creates new jobs at suppliers who support the plant's operations and in the surrounding communities where the plant workers will live and spend money from their high paying jobs. Marysville in Union County, Ohio is a great illustration of this. Within 10 years of the opening of the Honda plant in that region, per capita income more than doubled, housing starts increased almost twenty times and storefront vacancies became nonexistent[76].

In the nineties, high tech industries emerged as the primary source of the anchor jobs and the multiplier effect for these jobs was larger than for manufacturing jobs. As a matter of fact, there were several studies during the nineties and early in the new millennium that discussed the multiplier effect of high-tech jobs and they showed that the California "two for one" estimate is certainly plausible to apply the national economy and might be even a bit conservative. In Pennsylvania's Technology 21 report, the job multiplier effect is estimated at 1.5 to 2.0 for traditional industries[77]. Meanwhile, one study conducted to assess the impact of Microsoft on the Washington state economy estimated that for each Microsoft job created, nearly seven (6.7) additional jobs were created in the state[78]. Another study conducted to assess the impact of building a nationwide broadband network estimated the employment multiplier effect at 4.1 indirect jobs for every direct job created by this investment[79].

Taking into account the employment multiplier effect, a straightforward conclusion is that a substantial percentage of the job creation during the nineties can be credited to the emergence of the Internet economy, perhaps as much as 50 percent. If the Clinton administration is to take credit for the jobs created by the internet economy, it has to be demonstrated that the administration had a major role in the Internet's transformation from a medium for academics, nerds and national security operatives to an engine for business and commerce. Members of the administration can certainly be credited with pro-Internet rhetoric, but actual policy moves that aided the growth of the Internet are at best difficult to find.

More Ripple Effects of the Internet Economy

The impact of the Internet extended to other aspects of the economy as well. Not only was Netscape the catalyst that helped drive widespread adoption of the Internet, it also turned out to be the catalyst that energized investment in Internet related companies. Its Initial Public Offering (IPO) of stocks for sale to the public was the first of a plethora of runaway IPO's. Netscape originally proposed to offer 3.5 million shares of stock at $12 to $14 a share. It eventually offered 5 million shares at $28 a share and the stock actually wound up opening at $71 a share[80]. Even with the additional shares added to the offering, Fortune magazine reported that the IPO was oversubscribed by as much as 100 million shares[81].

This marked the beginning of a torrid IPO market that created a bumper crop of instant millionaires and billionaires. In 1995 alone nearly $30 billion in new company stock was sold followed by $39 billion in 1996 and a peak of $62 billion in 1999[82]. The Netscape scenario was repeated many times over with companies like Yahoo, Excite, and Lycos. By 1999 it was pretty common for IPOs to double their offer price or better on the first day. In December of 1999, USA

Today reported that 105 of the 474 IPOs that had debuted during the year had doubled their offer price or better on their first day of trading[83]. At press time for the USA piece, on average, those IPOs had almost doubled again.

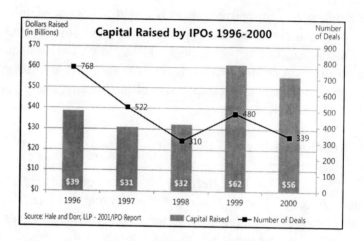

While much of this was focused on Internet related companies, the enthusiasm rubbed off on other companies as well and virtually every IPO became an overnight success. The phenomenal success of IPO's in turn piqued the interest of venture capitalist who poured money into Internet start-ups at an astounding rate. Venture capital (VC) funding, which totaled $5 billion in 1995, grew to over $100 billion in 2000. At the height of the frenzy, during the first quarter of 2000, VCs invested almost $25 billion in early stage companies. One estimate put VC funding at $166 billion for 1999 and 2000 alone[84].

The VC industry itself grew during this period. According to the New York Times, in 2000 alone 250 new VC funds were announced with commitments of $70 billion, including 18 funds with holdings of at least 1 billion each[85]. The combination of the spectacular IPO market and the VC funding it stimulated had a significant impact on jobs. A study conducted for the National Venture Capital Association (NVCA) by DRI-WEFA evaluated the impact of $273 billion of VC investments on jobs and gross domestic product since 1970[86]. It found that VC investing had created companies that were responsible for 7.6 million jobs and more than $1.3 trillion in revenue as of the end of 2000. This study covers a much larger span of time than this book is focused on so why bring it up? It turns out more than 80% of the $273 billion referenced in the study was spent during the nineties and particularly from 1995 to 2000, which would also put around 80% or about six million of the jobs created by these investments smack in the middle of the Clinton era. In fact, the NVCA study estimated that at the end of 2000, there were 1.4 million VC supported jobs in California alone.

The capital invested by VCs in turn generated more funds through IPOs and these funds contributed to job creation. Mark Lackritz, president of the Securities Industry Association in 1996, estimated that 750,000 jobs were created by the $30 billion raised in IPOs in 1995[87]. Meanwhile, $248 billion was raised in IPOs between 1995 and 2000. Using Mr. Lacritz's math, that would put IPO related jobs at 6.2 million. Both the NVCA study and Mr. Lacritz's projections were a bit generous in terms of the amount they estimated to be the unit cost for creating a single job coming in at $36k and $40k respectively. However, even if these two forces were credited with one half as many jobs as were estimated, their contribution to the nineties job count would still amount to about a quarter of the jobs created.

It is almost impossible to overstate the impact of the Web revolution on the prolonged economic expansion of the nineties. It infused the economy with cash. It generated jobs, direct and indirect. It propelled capital markets. It created buzz and excitement among business leaders, investors, and consumers. It supercharged real estate. In fact, its impact was so extensive that at times it was compared to a second industrial revolution. And it all came about as a result of private enterprise and the creative American spirit, not an economic stimulus plan hatched by politicians in Washington. Government did have a role as it funded research that resulted in the invention of one of the key components that launched the revolution, i.e., the browser. But, it was a matter of happenstance not purposeful policy making.

Chapter 4: The Telecom Act of 1996

✌:∼

Perhaps one of the most significant pieces of legislation passed during the '90s was the Telecom Act of 1996 (TA-96). The rules that governed the nation's communications policy had not been updated across-the-board since the Communications Act of 1934 and needed to be revised to account for the myriad of advancements in communications that had taken place since then. This became particularly apparent in the '90s with the emergence of the Internet as a major medium for communications. The need was also highlighted because of advancements in wireless communications and cable television, which had achieved critical mass in the marketplace.

TA-96 was designed to bring US communications policy in line with the requirements of the 21st century. In a nutshell it lifted restrictions that kept market leaders in one segment of the communications industry from competing with their counterparts in other segments of the industry and opened doors for completely new entrants to join the fray. Below are some of the key provisions of the bill[88]:

- Local telephone companies also known as local exchange carriers (LECs) were permitted to offer long distance service provided they met certain conditions to open up their networks to allow competitors to offer local service
- Incumbent local telephone companies (i.e., the Baby Bells) were required to work with any new local telephone companies to provide interconnection, number portability, dialing parity, and access to rights-of-way
- The Big Three long distance providers (AT&T, MCI and Sprint) and cable companies were permitted to offer local telephone service
- LECs were permitted to provide video programming within their local services areas. Previously, they had been permitted to offer video programming in other markets but not within their own footprint.
- Previous limits on national ownership for radio stations were eliminated and ownership rules for local stations were changed to allow a single company to own more stations
- The 12-station cap on television station ownership was eliminated and the allowed coverage limit was raised from 25% to 35%, meaning that a single broadcaster, no matter how many television stations are owned, can reach a maximum of 35% of the TV homes in the United States.

Phase 1 of telecommunications deregulation, which was launched by the breakup of AT&T on January 1, 1984, was frequently second guessed by skeptics who subscribed to a point of view along the lines of "If you've got the best telecommunications network in the world and it ain't broke, why fix it?" But 12 years into the "experiment" it was pretty clear that the break-up of AT&T had produced a lot of positive benefits. As a result, when the Telecom Act of 1996 (TA-96) was passed, visionaries, entrepreneurs, investors, consumers, and other stakeholders were already lined up to take advantage of the next wave of telecommunications deregulation.

Without a doubt, the breakup of AT&T in 1984 took a lot of getting used to, but when the dust had settled 12 years later it had produced a number of desirable outcomes, including the following:

- **Telecommunications innovation** — At the time of the AT&T break up in 1984, telecommunications was still very much about transporting voice from one point to another and phones were still very much dumb instruments used to make and receive calls. By 1995 the industry was fundamentally changed. Phones were becoming a productivity tool in addition to a conversation tool. Wireless phones had erased the boundaries that defined places of business and made it possible to conduct business from practically anywhere. Conference calling made it possible to conduct meetings with multiple parties without having to bring them together physically in the same room thus enabling business transactions. Voicemail freed up administrative assistants from message taking to focus on higher value activities. Toll-free calling offered businesses a new paradigm for reaching customers. Custom calling features like call waiting, call forwarding, caller-ID, and return call added completely new dimensions to how consumers used their phones. And the list goes on.
- **Fortune 500 long distance competitors** — Before the long distance market was opened to competition in 1984 MCI was a blip on the corporate radar screen at merely $100,000 in revenue in 1978[89]. By 1995 it was a $13.3 billion company[90]. Similarly, in 1984

Sprint, which was a division of GTE, had around $1 billion in revenues[91]. By 1995 it was a $12.6 billion company[92].

- **Truly competitive long distance market** — Prior to the break-up of AT&T in 1984, the company was in virtually complete control of the telecommunications market in the US, long distance included. For all practical purposes, it was the only game in town. By 1995 there were as many as 500[93] companies offering long distance service. Some would argue (and several did) that most of these companies were not viable competitors to AT&T and that though there was a plethora of service providers to choose from, the market was not really competitive. But, one tell-tale sign that real competition in the long distance space had emerged was that AT&T's market share had declined from 84% in 1984 to 56% in 1995[94].

  Another telltale sign of competition was how AT&T invested its money. For example, in 1985 AT&T had 136,000 miles of fiber optic cable deployed in its network. MCI and Sprint had a combined total of 206,000 miles of fiber deployed[95]. However, early on in the competition for long distance customers Sprint promoted its network quality as a differentiator with its "Pin drop" marketing campaign and announced its plans to build the first all fiber optic network. With competitive challenges like this as an incentive, by 1994 AT&T had upped its deployment of fiber to 1.2 million miles[96].

- **Better long distance prices for consumers** — Estimates vary on how much long distance rates decreased between 1984 and 1995 ranging from 30%[97] to 65%[98], but regardless of which end of the range one accepts, the savings to the public are substantial. During the eighties and the nineties, if you watched TV or listened to the radio, there was no escaping the ad wars between the market share leaders in long distance telecommunications, i.e., AT&T, MCI, and Sprint. Occasionally long distance ads appealed to the public on the basis of who had the better network or who had the better track record delivering long distance service to the public, but the most prominent subject of long distance ads was who was offering better prices.

Each one of the Big Three was constantly coming up with creative marketing programs to lure customers away from the others (or to keep them from defecting to the others). Among the better known ones were programs like AT&T One Rate, MCI Friends and Family, and Sprint Sense. The ad wars extended to competition for carrying customers' collect calls. MCI launched the war with its offering of 1-800-COLLECT and AT&T responded first with 1-800-OPERATOR then 1-800-CALL-ATT. Once again it was all about price and the public was the beneficiary.

By 1996 the Big Three were offering flat rate plans for as low as 10¢ -15¢ per minute to anywhere in the country. Meanwhile, in 1984 the standard rate for a call between locations 1900 plus miles apart was 74¢ per minute for the first minute and 49¢ per minute for each additional minute[99]. In a speech to the national press club in February of 2000, FCC Chairman Kennard estimated the public had saved $200 billion since the break-up of AT&T[100].

With the dramatic decrease in the price of long distance calls came a dramatic increase in the number of long distance minutes consumed by the public as Americans fundamentally changed the way they used their phones to keep in touch with one another. Calls that were once reserved for special occasions became commonplace. Between 1984 and 1994 consumption of interstate long distance minutes increased by 2.5 times from 169 billion minutes to 424 billion minutes, and intrastate long distance doubled growing from 166 billion minutes to 331 billion minutes[101]. Another measure that shows the dramatic increase in phone usage as a result of better prices is the number of daily conversations conducted by Americans on the phone. According to the Census Bureau reports, between 1984 and 1995 daily conversations grew from 1.2 billion to 11.6 billion, an increase of almost tenfold[102].

- **Creation of shareholder value** — At the time of the initial deregulation, AT&T had a market capitalization of $59 billion[103] and was the largest company in the world with more than one million employees[104]. By 1996 the combined market value of the top 14 players in the telecommunications market was $338 billion[105].

- **New industries** — The prepaid calling card industry did not exist before the first round of telecommunications deregulation in 1984, but by 1996 it was producing more than a billion in revenues[106]. Wholesale long distance also did not exist prior to the AT&T breakup in 1984, but by 1995, switch-less resale of long distance services was a $60 billion business[107].

When the Telecom Act of 1996 was passed, everyone was ready for more of the same. TA-96 never did deliver the competitive local phone market that was envisioned. But for a short period from 1996 - 2001, it generated an extraordinary amount of economic activity. For example, TA-96 was responsible for the birth of a large number of new telecommunications companies, commonly referred to as (CLECs) Competitive Local Exchange Carriers and Data Local Exchange Carriers (DLECs). These companies were formed to take advantage of the provision in TA-96 that opened up local telephone service to competition in a similar way to how the original breakup of AT&T opened up the long distance market to competition. Before the Telecom Act of 1996 there were 13 competitive facilities-based carriers, i.e., carriers with their own network facilities. Two years after the passage of the TA-96 there were 160, and by early 2000 there were 333[108]. In 1996 there were nine publicly traded competitive carriers with a combined market capitalization of $3.1 billion. By early 2000, there were 35 publicly traded Competitive Local Exchange Carriers (CLECs) with a combined market capitalization of $86.4 billion[109].

TA-96 also ignited an enormous amount of investment in telecommunications infrastructure. The year-over-year increase in capital expenditures in the communications industry from 1994 to 1995 was practically flat with the '94 figure standing at $37 billion and the '95 figure at $38 billion. Then the Telecom Act of 1996 was passed into law on February 8, 1996. The very same year communications industry capital expenditures grew by 26% to $48 billion, and from 1996 through 2000, communications industry capital expenditures grew every year by at least 19% and sometimes by as much as 36%. By 2000, capital expenditures for the industry stood at $135 billion, which is nearly quadruple what it was before passage of the Telecom Act of 1996. Overall from 1996 through 2000 capital expenditures in the communications industry in the US amounted to $530 billion[110].

This extraordinary growth was not all due to TA-96. As you know from earlier portions of this book, this period of growth coincides with the Internet boom, which also had an impact on communications industry capital expenditures.

However, an analysis of TA-'96 related capital expenditures puts the figure at $150 billion over the period 1996 – 2001[111].

In addition to the new competitive carriers that were launched in response to TA-96, the law was also the impetus for the creation or growth of a sizeable number of software companies. These companies were formed to tackle the operational support system requirements of the law as well as those of the new competitive carriers. Operational Support Systems (OSSs) are the software systems that communications companies use to take orders, assign physical resources like access lines, manage networks, and bill for service. One example of an OSS requirement driven by TA-96 was Local Number Portability (LNP), i.e., the ability for a customer to change their local telephone provider without having to change their telephone number. Another OSS requirement driven by TA-96 was the need for the RBOCs to provide competitors with access to their Operational Support Systems. These and other OSS requirements drove the need for incumbents and new entrants alike to invest in OSSs. By 2001there were approximately 200 OSS vendors in business together with another 200 involved in some aspect of billing software[112].

Given the explosion in the number of new companies being created as well as the extraordinary acceleration in the amount of investment in capital equipment, one might expect that a by-product of this activity would be new jobs. The jobs data from that period indicates that this hypothesis is spot on.

An analysis by the bureau of Labor statistics[113] shows that during the first few years of the '90s, the telecommunications industry actually lost 43,000 jobs. The next three years were characterized by modest job growth of approximately 12,000 jobs per year. However, in the 1996, the year TA-96 was passed, the industry added 43,000 jobs. The next year job growth increased again to 62,000 jobs. In 2000 job growth peaked at 104,000 jobs, almost nine times the average number of jobs created during the first three years of the Clinton administration. Overall during the five-year period from January 1996 to March 2001 the industry gained 352,000 jobs. These statistics definitely suggest a connection between the passage of TA-96 and the acceleration of job creation in the telecommunications industry during the nineties.

Any doubt that TA-96 was the catalyst for this extraordinary job growth can be removed by taking a look at what happened when investments in local exchange carrier start-ups and capital fueled by TA-96 suddenly came to a halt in 2001. After six interest rate increases over an 18-month period as well as the Dot-com bust, the requirements for obtaining investment capital for new ventures tightened significantly and the flow of dollars into fledgling start-up businesses slowed tremendously. The scarcity of capital exposed the flaws in the business models of the CLECs and DLECs and soon not only were there essentially no new investments in CLECs and DLECs, many of the existing ones were declaring bankruptcy and shutting down operations.

The subsequent job losses were just as spectacular as the increases that were seen following the passage of TA-96. Between March 2001 and December 2001 the industry lost 72,000 jobs. In the following 12 months, the industry lost another 130,000 jobs. By December of 2005 the industry had lost 337,000 jobs from its peak in March 2001[114].

So job growth in the industry accelerated soon after TA-96 was passed and it declined soon after it became apparent one of the key paradigms for local telephone competition that the bill's architects envisioned wasn't working. Was there a cause and effect relationship between TA-96 and job growth in the nineties? You make the call.

Remember the job multiplier effect discussed in the chapter about the Internet economy? It applies here too. The impact of TA-96 on job creation was not limited to creation of direct telecommunication industry jobs. In a progress report on the telecommunications industry released in early 1999, President Clinton's Council of Economic Advisors estimated that three plus jobs were created in other industries for every job created in the telecommunications industry between 1993 and 1998[115]. The report also cited statistics from the Cellular Telephone Industry Association showing that 130,000 direct jobs at wireless carriers translated to 260,000 sales and distribution jobs, 45,000 manufacturing jobs, and over 600,000 support service, construction and product development jobs related to wireless. These figures might be a bit optimistic, but the principle of multiplier effects for wireless communications jobs comes through loud and clear. Moreover, similar multiplier effects existed in all sectors of the telecommunications industry.

To finish up this section, we need to add one final note about the economic activity unleashed by TA-96, that is, it was not limited to traditional telecommunications entities. You might recall that the bill had provisions that addressed radio and television station ownership. It turns out that among the first to capitalize on the new freedoms provided by the bill were broadcast conglomerates like Triathlon Broadcasting, which laid out $37 million to purchase seven stations and Jacor Communications that bought Citicasters for $770 million as well as Noble Broadcast group for $152 million[116].

Telecom Act of 1996: Brain Child of the Clinton Administration?

The Telecom Act of 1996 represents yet another phenomenon that poured hundreds of billions of dollars into the economy during the period 1996 — 2001; the other two mentioned so far being the Y2K remediation problem and the Internet boom. This time the federal government played a direct role by passing a law that removed some obstacles to competition in the telecommunications industry. Perhaps in this case the Clinton administration is well positioned to take credit for this economic stimulus. After all it came about as a result of a law that was passed on President Clinton's watch. However, a review of the events leading up to the passage of this bill paints a very different picture.

The Telecom Act of 1996 was not a key part of the Clinton legislative agenda. Instead, it was part of a legislative agenda that gained momentum after Republicans took control of Congress following the mid-term elections of 1994. This particular aspect of the Republican agenda was not too popular with the President and Congressional Democrats either. When the bill initially started making its way through Congress, Clinton threatened to veto it. When it was nearing its passage in the Senate, Bob Kerrey threatened to filibuster it. In the June 9, 1995 edition of the New York Times Senator Kerrey is quoted as follows[117]:

"This bill is a contract with corporations in America, maybe 100 corporations. It is not a contract with America and American people have not been asking for it."

To be fair, the Telecom Act of 1996 had no shortage of opponents or supporters. It was also opposed by long distance companies like AT&T, MCI, and Sprint as well as consumer groups like the Consumer Federation of America. There were two main complaints against the bill. First, opponents were concerned that it did not do enough to ensure that in a deregulated environment the Regional Bells could not use their existing monopolies to stifle competition. Second there was a concern that a provision in the bill which removed certain restrictions on ownership of media would allow control of media to be concentrated in the hands of a few powerful people, which in turn could lead to restriction in the marketplace of ideas. However, the bill's sponsors worked tirelessly to build consensus and secure agreements among interested parties that would make it possible to pass the bill.

A telecommunications reform bill had originally been introduced by Senator Ernest Hollings (Dem., SC) and John Danforth (Rep. MO) in February of 1994, but that bill died without ever coming to a vote due in part to opposition from the Regional Bell Operating Companies. The knock on the Hollings bill was that it still contained too many regulatory requirements to open the market up to competition. Despite a fair amount of negotiation the bill never garnered the type of broad-based support in Congress or within the business community that it needed to pass.

When the Hollings bill was in play, the President's Council of Economic Advisers had released a briefing paper including forecasts that deregulation of the telecommunications industry would boost America's global competitiveness and produce 1.4 million jobs by 2003[118]. Yet, according to the Los Angeles times, the bill did not enjoy the type of high-profile support from the White House that was given to the North American Free Trade Agreement.

> But on Capitol Hill, telecom reform has been eclipsed by the health care debate, and it lacks the high-profile White House support that the North American Free Trade Agreement enjoyed.
>
> Los Angeles Times
> August, 1994

This is the type of support that includes frequent references to the bill in public forums, summoning congressional leaders to White House for gentle arm twisting or deal making, and meetings with business leaders to gain their support. Presidents have been known to do this of thing for bills they really care about. In the case of the Hollings bill, the White House was content to sit on the sidelines and let it die.

When all is said and done, Clinton did not introduce the bill. He wasn't particularly supportive of it. Now that in retrospect it is clear that TA-96 had a significant impact on the economy of the 1990s he cannot take credit for it.

Of course this does not mean that the administration wouldn't try. A review of the literature will show attempts of the administration to try to tie TA-96 to the National Information Infrastructure (NII) vision that was unveiled early during the Clinton administration. For example, a report from the president's Council of Economic Advisors (CEA) in 1999 describes five principles that the NII advanced as a framework for formulating legislation around regulatory reform[119]:

- Encouraging private investment in information infrastructure
- Promoting and protecting competition
- Providing open access to advanced telecommunications networks for consumers and service providers
- Preserving and advancing universal service to avoid creating a society of information "haves" and "have nots"
- Ensuring flexibility so that the newly-adopted regulatory framework can adapt to rapid technological and market changes in the telecommunications and information industries

But does the nineties' landmark telecommunications bill really have its foundations in NII? When a comparison is made between these principles and the major provisions of TA-96 presented earlier it is a stretch to find a connection between the two. Even the CEA was careful to say "The principles of the NII initiative are reflected in many instances in the Telecommunications Act of 1996" not something like the Telecom Act of 1996 was built around the NII principles. The notion that TA-96 originated with NII is about as credible as the notion that Al Gore invented the Internet.

The Impact of International Deregulation

Another aspect of telecommunications deregulation that had an impact on the US economy was liberalization of telecommunications networks around the world particularly in Europe and Asia. Major developments in deregulation of international telecommunications markets took place around the same time that the US market was deregulated and produced similar results in terms of capital expenditures. For example, in the early 1990s, the European Union had set a timetable for telecommunications markets to be deregulated by 1998[120].

According to a 2001 report by the Organization for Economic Co-Operation and Development (OECD), telecommunications capital spending among OECD member countries in 1999 was $200 billion, which represented a 19% increase over 1998 and a 32% increase over 1997[121]. This confirms that not only was investment in telecommunications infrastructure increasing in the US, it was also increasing around the world. One might ask "What does this have to do with the US economy?"

First, telecommunications deregulation gave momentum to the concept of the Global carrier. The top telecommunications carriers worldwide not only positioned themselves to be competitive in their own markets but also in key markets around the world, the US being the biggest prize. As a result a fair amount of capital spending was directed at the US by offshore companies. Hard numbers on the size of these investments are hard to come by, but an illustration in the OECD report sheds some light on how this worked out. 360Networks projected capital expenditures of $2.8 billion of which $1.2 billion would be spent in North America[122].

Another reason why the US economy benefited from international telecommunications deregulation was because US vendors like Cisco Systems and Juniper Networks were the suppliers of many of the technologies that were used to modernize incumbent telecommunications networks or build new entrant networks. In 1999 new entrants were responsible for 35% of capital equipment expenditures in OECD markets and it showed up in the financials of these companies. For example, between 1995 and 2000, sales for network equipment manufacturer Cisco Systems grew from $2.2 billion to $18.9 billion. In 1999, about one third of Cisco sales were made to customers outside of the U.S. Whereas at the beginning of the nineties Japan was the leading exporter of communications equipment with exports totaling $11.6 billion and the U.S. had exports of less than $10 billion[123], by 2000 the U.S. had emerged as the leading exporter of communications equipment with exports of $28.4 billion[124].

To close out this section, it is important to point out that the boom in economic activity that was ignited by TA-96 was followed by an equally if not more spectacular bust. For example, by August 2002 the popular press (vs. the Bureau of Labor Statistics) was reporting that the telecom industry had lost 500,000 jobs[125], by some accounts more jobs than it had created in the five years immediately following passage of the telecom act. It did not produce the competition in local telephone service that was envisioned by its sponsors. Real competition in local telephone service came from elsewhere, i.e., the emergence of Voice over IP as a viable alternative to traditional telephone service. As a result, there is no shortage of detractors for this piece of legislation. Be that as it may, this does not change the fact that even though its positive economic impact was short lived; TA-96 was indeed one of the forces that was at work during the economic perfect storm of the '90s.

The purpose of this section was not to hail TA-96 as the best legislation for Phase 2 of deregulating the telecommunications industry. Instead its focus is limited to how TA-96 impacted the '90s economy and who should take credit or blame for that. Some perspectives on TA-96 effectiveness as a framework for deregulation will be addressed in another section of the book.

Chapter 5: Cheap Money

⌣∴⌣

"After more than two years of sputtering and hesita-
tion, the U.S. economy is finally beginning to act the
way it's supposed to. ... The magic elixir giving the
economy a much healthier and more robust step? The
lowest interest rates in more than two decades."[126]

Lucinda Harper and Erle Norton
Washington Post
December, 1993

When Bill Clinton took office in January of 1993, he
inherited an economic environment that was already
headed in the right direction as a result of momentum from
four interest rate cuts by the Federal Reserve Board in 1992.
By the time of Clinton's inauguration, the economy had
already grown for three consecutive quarters and generated
450,000 jobs[127] in the previous twelve months; anemic job
growth as compared with previous post-recession recoveries
but a positive trajectory nevertheless. Overall GDP growth
for the year, though sluggish at times, was 2.6%[128], including
a whopping 5.7% for the fourth quarter[129]. Lest you dismiss
this as a "gimme", i.e., every president gets to benefit a bit
from his predecessor's coattails, consider the economic

environment George W. Bush inherited when he took office in January of 2001:

- Interest rates had been raised six times in the previous 18 months[130]
- The high flying NASDAQ had lost 39 percent of its value and the S&P 500 had lost 10 percent of its value[131]
- Real GDP had shrunk from 4.8% in the first quarter of 2000 to 1% in fourth quarter of 2000[132]
- Business investment had shrunk from 20.6% to -3.3%[133]
- Job growth had slowed significantly[134].

Economic indicators were all pointing toward recession, and that is exactly what followed.

Similarly consider the prevailing economic conditions when Ronald Reagan took office in January of 1981[135]:

- Interest rates were as high as 21%
- Unemployment stood at 7.5%
- Inflation had risen to 12.5%

The upshot of this is that presidents do not always benefit from their predecessor's coattails. Sometimes they are actually handicapped by them. With that in mind, it is significant that at the time of his ascension to office, Bill Clinton was the beneficiary of a favorable monetary environment that he did not help to create, and that he was already ahead of the curve on inauguration day instead of being behind the eight ball. The cost of borrowing money was relatively cheap compared to the 80s and it remained that way throughout the period.

The US economy, by far the largest in the world, is complex and numerous factors affect its movement in one direction or another. However, some economic cause and effect relationships are relatively straight forward. For example, a substantial reduction in interest rates or atypically low interest rates (e.g., lowest in 20 years or so) generally translate to increased home sales and significant mortgage refinancing activity, which in turn translate into construction jobs. Evidence of this is provided by the fact that home sales, mortgage refinancing and construction activity held their own from 2001-2004 despite one of the deepest economic down turns the country has ever experienced. During that same period interest rates remained at historic lows the likes of which had not been seen for 40 years.

What does this have to do with the '90s economic boom: quite a lot actually. One of the strongest segments of the economy during the 1990s was construction. Between 1993 and 2000, the construction industry produced around 2,000,000 jobs. This industry was already on the move by the time Bill Clinton came to office and benefited throughout his administration from interest rates which for the most part remained at historic lows. True the interest rates of the 90s were not as low as the interest rates in the early part of the new millennium, but comparatively speaking, they were low enough to fuel substantial economic activity in the construction and construction finance sectors of the economy.

It would be wrong to suggest that the Clinton administration did not have any positive impact on monetary policy once in office. Three specific items either embraced or driven by the administration had a positive effect on monetary policy: 1) Congress' adoption of a practice of identifying how programs or tax cuts would be paid for before passing related legislation, sometimes referred to as the doctrine of fiscal discipline, 2) Initial efforts by the administration to reduce deficit spending, and 3) Systematic reduction in the size of the federal government, which manifested itself in a reduction in the number of federal workers.

However the monetary policy that made cheap money accessible to consumers and businesses was already in place by the time the Clinton administration began and had already begun to generate positive results for the economy. Some sectors of the economy are particularly sensitive to the cost of money, e.g., home sales, mortgage refinancing, construction, capital equipment expenditures. These sectors turned the corner or began turning the corner in 1992 when the cost of money hit a critical threshold and then thrived throughout the 90's as the cost of money remained cheap.

A President's Dream: Tax Cuts and Deficit Reduction without an Act of Congress

One notable example of this phenomenon is mortgage refinancing. Mortgage rates hit an inflection point in 1992. They reached 15-year then 19-year[136] lows setting off two booms in mortgage refinancing with the second continuing on into 1993. As a result of interest rate reductions, it was estimated that the potential market for mortgage refinancing was $800 billion and homeowners jumped on the opportunity to the tune of $400 billion worth of refinanced mortgages in 1992[137].

This is significant as concerns economic momentum for several reasons. First, the fundamentals which drove the hyper growth in mortgage refinancing activity were so firmly established that the refinancing boom was poised to continue into 1993 regardless of who won the 1992 elections. In fact, in its October 19, 1992 issue, the Wall Street Journal advanced this very point of view in an article entitled **"Mortgage Refinancing Boom is Expected to Continue Whoever Wins the Election."** True to form, the refinancing boom did continue into 1993 as another $560 billion[138] in residential mortgage loans were refinanced.

Second, the refinancing boom put a lot of extra dollars in homeowners' pockets. In July 1992, when the boom was still underway, the Mortgage Bankers Association of America (MBA) estimated that as a result of refinancing, homeowners would have as much as an additional $6 billion to spend[139]. That's a pretty good chunk of change in an economy where consumer spending accounts for two-thirds of economic activity.

However, after the boom had run its course and more comprehensive estimates became available, it became clear that the economic impact of refinancing was by far higher. According to David Berson of the Federal National Mortgage Association, in just '93 alone the amount homeowners saved was around $20 billion[140]. Meanwhile, James Chessen, chief economist of the American Bankers Association, estimated the economic impact of the '92-'93 boom at $40 billion[141]. Still another prominent economist, Henry Kaufman, gave a speech in 1995 looking back at the boom of 1992-1993 where he stated "We have estimated that the cumulative effect of this refinancing was the equivalent of a $100 billion tax cut for the household sector, surely a source of ongoing stimulus for the economy[142]."

Regardless of whether one chooses to go with the low end or the high end of these estimates we're talking pretty substantial economic stimulus, in every case bigger than what the President himself had proposed. Imagine being president and having the luxury of giving the electorate a tax cut that large without having to enact legislation to do it. That's exactly what mortgage refinancing gave Bill Clinton.

The refinancing boom had still another by-product that contributed to positive economic momentum: lower mortgage interest rate deductions on tax returns. As homeowners lowered their mortgage interest rates, they also reduced the amount of interest they would be able deduct on their tax returns to decrease their taxable incomes. Smaller mortgage interest rate deductions translate to higher tax revenues, which in turn translates to reductions in the federal budget deficit.

Indeed experts did estimate that mortgage refinancing helped to cut the budget deficit a bit in 1993. According to an article in National Mortgage News in May 1995, IRS figures showed that 27 million taxpayers claimed $185.6 billion in home mortgage interest deductions in 1993 as compared with $198 billion claimed by 27 million taxpayers in 1992.[143]

Right about now you're thinking "This writer's talking out of both sides of his mouth. You can't have a tax cut and a tax increase at the same time." That's right! You can't!! So to make sense of what has just been described, there are two things you need to keep in mind:

1. There wasn't actually a tax cut. Economists only compared the amount of money that refinancing put back into homeowners' pockets to a tax cut.
2. Homeowners had to give back some of their savings in taxes, but the net positive impact to their pocket-books was still huge.

To sum up what has been shared so far regarding this first example of the cheap money phenomenon in the nineties, the flood of refinancing that occurred from early '92 through early '94 had a doubly positive effect on the economy (more spending money for families and more revenue for the government), it was launched before the beginning of the Clinton presidency and was driven by forces that had little to do with his policies.

Déjà vu All over Again

The refinancing frenzy repeated itself again in the '97-'99 time frame. Once again the million dollar question is whether administration policies were the primary driver of falling interest rates or were rate reductions driven by something else.

The second boom was even stronger than the first because in addition to the first time refinancers, the '92-'93 wave of refinancing had created a pool of experienced homeowners who were savvy about issues like what interest rate thresholds should be the trigger for refinancing their loans, what benefits could be obtained from refinancing as well as what is the process involved in getting a mortgage refinanced. Homeowners were also more sophisticated about their reasons for refinancing. During the '92-'93 boom it was all about reducing mortgage payments, but in the '97-'99 wave, reasons included funding major home improvements, financing children's college education, consolidation of credit card debt to obtain lower interest rates as well as tax benefits, and creation of additional wealth through lucrative investments.

Lenders were also more prepared the second time around. This time they helped to drive the market by creating new programs and soliciting borrowers through direct mail campaigns. Some lenders began to offer refinancing deals with minimal fees and no points, which expanded the base of homeowners who could benefit from restructuring their mortgages.

In the wake of the '92-'93 boom, Fannie Mae's chief economist, David Berson, had predicted that even when the refinancing booms had abated, there would be more refinancing than there had been historically, i.e., there would be a "new normal" level for refinancing. What were his reasons?

"The underlying rate of mortgage refinancing will move up modestly from their historical levels for two reasons: first, because of the prevalence of low- and no-cost refinancing and psychologically, because so many people have refinanced, it will be an easier thing for everyone to do in the future. You did it, you survived it, it wasn't so bad, so maybe you'll do it again if conditions warrant.[144]"

It turns out Berson was right, only the catalysts he cited didn't just contribute to a new higher normal level of refinancing; they helped push refinancing rates to all time highs and poured tens of billions of dollars into the economy during '97-'99 refinancing cycle. Here are some statistics on Refinancing Wave 2.

- An estimated 22 million[145] mortgage holders were positioned to benefit from refinancing versus 6 million in the previous wave. Put another way, about half of all mortgage holders could benefit from refinancing versus one third during the previous wave[146].
- The refinancing index is a metric published by the Mortgage Bankers Association of America that gauges the volume of refinancing activity in the home lending market. During the '97-'99 refinancing cycle the refinancing index peaked at 4389. The previous peak during the '92-'93 boom was 1838[147].
- $735 billion in mortgages was refinanced in 1998[148] eclipsing the previous record of $560 billion in 1993.
- $54 billion of equity was withdrawn 1998-1999, including $18 billion spent on home improvements, $15 billion spent on paying off higher interest debts, $10 billion spent on real estate or business investments, $10 billion in basic consumer spending, and $1 billion funneled into stock market investments[149].

Clearly refinancing driven by low interest rates was as much of a boon for the economy in the '97-'99 time frame as it was during the early years of the Clinton administration.

Before leaving the subject of mortgage refinancing, it's worth recapping a few takeaways regarding the relationship between interest rates and this powerful phenomenon:

1. Refinancing patterns in 1992 illustrate just how sensitive this market is to interest rates. The mortgage refinancing boom was completely driven by fluctuations in interest rates. Even in 1992 there were ebbs and flows in refinancing activity based on interest rates. In January of 1992 interest rates reached their lowest point in 15 years. The same month the MBA's index of refinancing applications peaked at 1428 and refinancing accounted for 73% of mortgage applications[150].

   However, as mortgage rates edged up during the first half of '92 the refinance index dropped to as low as 300 in June[151]. In early July the Federal Reserve cut rates and the index once again rose above 1000 (up to 1354 by July 24[152]) and stayed there for 12 straight weeks[153]. This whole cycle repeated itself as interest rates rose by half a percentage point and then fell again in the November '92 — early January '93 time frame.

   The strength of the relationship between mortgage refinancing and mortgage interest rates is even clearer when they are plotted versus one another on a graph. Below are three graphs which plot the mortgage refinance index versus 30-year mortgage interest rates for selected periods; two covering the period between September 1991 and September 1993 and one covering the period September 1997 to June 1998. Upon reviewing these charts, the strong relationship between mortgage refinancing and mortgage interest rates is unmistakable. Three takeaways emerge from inspection of the graphs: 1) In general, refinancing tends to go up as interest rates go down and vice versa, 2) Certain interest rate thresholds induce spikes in refinancing activity, 3) Once interest rates bottom out and start to go up, refinancing slows down until a series of consecutive rate reductions drive rates to a new threshold point.

2. The benefits of interest rate reductions were already taking hold in 1992. One indicator of this is that in the fourth quarter of 1992 late payments on residential mortgages dropped to their lowest level in 18 years[154].

3. The dip in interest rates to historically low levels was a disruptive influence on the home mortgage market in general and the refinancing market in particular. It unleashed a flood of new borrowers as well as lenders into the marketplace and with them new programs like "no closing cost" refinancing, lower or even no down payments for first mortgages, interest only mortgage payments, and so on. As a result, traditional rules of thumb regarding thresholds for refinancing like the homeowner's time horizon for living in the home or the rate reduction the homeowner hoped to achieve were thrown out of the window. Typically homeowners had been counseled to refinance only if they planned to stay in their homes for at least three to five additional years or if rates had dropped to at least

two percentage points below their existing mortgage rate. However, with the advent of programs enabling homeowners to refinance with no out of pocket costs, these rules no longer applied. Homeowners could refinance to take advantage of rate reductions of as little as half a point and they did. Homeowners sometimes refinanced multiple times within the space of a few months versus once in a long while, which had been the norm.

Cheap Money Lights a Fire in the Housing Market

Interest rates do not function like a light switch, i.e., you flick the interest rate switch and the economy immediately turns on. Instead, they function more like the embers that sometimes start a forest fire. With a little bit of fanning the embers ignite one combustible item then another and another. Pretty soon you have a full fledged fire going that defies containment and consumes acre after acre with seemingly no end in sight.

It's relatively easy to relate to the latter part of this analogy because once the economy got going in the '90s it seemed like the economic expansion would continue endlessly. We are however, less familiar with the front end, i.e., the gradual ignition of the economy by interest rates as they ignite mortgage refinancing then home sales then business investment in capital equipment and so on. But, it doesn't take a lot of thought or observation to realize that this does make sense.

Would-be homeowners don't go out and buy a house immediately after the first reduction in interest rates. Instead they try to wait for rates to bottom out so that they can get the best deal. After a down period in the housing market, developers don't immediately begin new projects at the first news of an interest rate cut. They wait a bit to be sure that the change will stick and that it will be incentive enough for buyers to start coming back into the market in sufficient numbers to make it worth their while.

This phenomenon is important because even though the conditions that set the stage for prolonged economic expansion were in place by the end of '92, some effects didn't fully take hold until the following year. All aspects of the turnaround were not quick starters like refinancing even though they showed signs of life in '92.

Housing construction and sales is an example of a sector of the economy that was stimulated by low interest rates but that took a while for its full impact to be felt in the economy. As with mortgage refinancing, the fundamentals of this sector had taken a sharp turn for the better well before Clinton took office. In '92 housing starts were up 18%[155], which is modest by comparison to other upturns in housing starts that occurred as the economy was emerging out of a recession but substantial nevertheless. It is also the largest single increase in housing starts for any year during the '90s.

However, even though ninety-three was also an up year for housing starts, it wasn't a straight line up. Housing starts alternated between peaks (hot) and valleys (cold) throughout the year as prospective home buyers timed the interest rate market to catch rates at their lowest point then rushed to take advantage of bargains at the first sign of an upturn in rates. Those who hadn't caught one wave of low rates waited for the next rate cut and jumped in when they thought it was just the right moment to get their best deal. Overall year housing starts for '93 were up 7% versus '92[156]. Even though the year-over-year increase was smaller than in '92, it was enough to drive the market to the threshold where it had enough momentum to spill over into other sectors of the economy.

By the end of '93 results were up for the home improvement industry, including household appliances, furniture and lumber to name a few. Overall, for 1993 the industry recorded a 9.8% increase in sales[157], and near the end of the year, sales of home improvement items were growing at roughly double[158] the rate of retail sales in general. The momentum in this sector was clearly linked to activity in the home construction and sales markets as is indicated by the following comments from industry executives and analysts.

"When you sell a home, you fix it up and when you buy one, you fix it up to meet your own tastes"[159]

John W. Hechinger Jr.
Chairman, Hechinger Co.
Wall Street Journal, December 1993

"When existing homes change hands, they are often renovated twice: superficially by the seller and seriously by the buyer."[160]

Ray Wise
Pension World, January 1994

"Seventy percent of such major household expenditures are made within the first few months after a home is bought."[161]

Mark Zandi
Chief Economist, Regional Financial Associate
Fortune, September 1994

Housing starts were strong again in ninety-four, up 13% and were up for six of the eight years from 1992 to 1999 while flat in the other two[162]. Time and again leading economists cited interest rates as the most important factor driving the housing market

On the August 1993 surge in housing starts
"Clearly interest rates were the dominant factor. Job growth is still slow. Household formation is still slow"[163]

David Seiders
Economist, NHBA
Seattle Post Intelligencer, September 1993

"Low interest rates are one of the strongest things the U.S. economy has going for it."[164]

Mark Obrinsky
Sr. Economist, FNMA
Wall Street Journal, December 1993

Housing starts are particularly pertinent to an understanding of the Clinton era economy because they tie directly to jobs. One housing industry executive, Roger Blunt (president of the National Association of Home Builders in 1993), put it this way: every 100,000 housing starts equates to 175,000 jobs[165]. Meanwhile, the strength of the housing market during the '90s tied directly to affordability and affordability tied directly to interest rates.

Sales of existing homes also responded to interest rates in '92 and were up almost 9% over the previous year[166]. This was a bigger increase than in 1993 and the third best showing for the period from 1991 — 2000. Twice during this period, in 1995 and 2000, sales of existing homes contracted for the year. In each case, the year with the dip was preceded by a year where interest rates were up overall. The following chart illustrates the relationship between interest rates and sales of existing homes:

Source: HUD (Sales) and MBA (Rates)

So the housing market didn't spring to life all at once, but the connection between interest rates and its rebirth in the '93-'94 time frame is unmistakable. The fact that the trigger point for this rebirth occurred in '92 is also unmistakable.

Capital Investments Get a Shot in the Arm from Cheap Money

Under the right conditions, cheap money (a.k.a. low interest rates) can have a pervasive impact on the economy. We have already seen that conditions were right in '92-'93 and in '97-'99 for interest rates to spark a boom in refinancing as well as a rebound in housing construction, home sales, and their related industries.

Low interest rates can also be a powerful stimulant for business investment in capital equipment. The rationale for this is pretty straight forward. When interest rates are high, banks can obtain adequate returns by investing in conservative instruments like government securities. But, in a low interest-rate environment, banks have to resort to other types of investments to boost their returns. Among these are loans to small and midsize companies that would normally be considered too high risk. These companies in turn use this cash to fund investments in capital equipment to improve productivity and grow their businesses.

In a low interest rate environment, individual investors also have to seek alternative investments to boost their returns. As a result, money flows to the stock market and direct investments in growing companies, providing businesses with the cash they need to make capital investments which enable growth.

This is all fine from a theoretical perspective, but did it actually pan out in real life? As a matter of fact, this was especially true in the nineties when computing resources, which were once reserved for the heavyweights of the business world, became accessible to average companies due to the ever increasing functionality as well as affordability of the personal computer. PCs also made computing power accessible to the average worker. From 1991 to 1992 businesses increased their spending on computer equipment by 70%[167]. In 1993 shipments of PCs to businesses ran about 40% ahead of 1992[168].

Even so, computers were not the only kind of capital equipment that thrived during this period. While several sectors of the economy that are typically strong during post-recession recoveries underperformed historic norms, capital equipment expenditures in the '91-'93 time frame outperformed results from previous recoveries. No matter which way the sector was looked at, there was good news to be found. Spending on durable equipment was up a respectable 7% for 1992[169] and a little more than double that (14.7%)[170] in 1993. In '94 it accounted for 8% of total economic output and 37% of the rise in GDP[171].

Several reasons were cited for the strength of the capital equipment sector, including the following[172]:

- The age of the nation's capital stock (the oldest it had been since 1945)
- Relative cost of machines to improve productivity versus hiring people
- Shifts or advancements in technology

However, one factor was a constant in every analyst's explanation of the capital phenomenon: low interest rates. In fact, in some sectors like automotive manufacturing and home goods manufacturing, the consumer demand that drove capital investments was directly related to low interest rates.

"Low interest rates are critical to business investment. When interest rates are high, businesses tend to repair old machinery, add labor instead of machinery or go out of business."

Jim Meil
Manager Economic Analysis, Eaton Corp.
Wall Street Journal, December 1993

"I give a lot of credit to interest rates"

James Dunstan
Chairman, Azon
Wall Street Journal, December 1993

"Lower interest rates are part of the reason demand for our goods is up."

Joseph G. Hill
CFO, DMI Furniture Inc.
Wall Street Journal, December 1993

When momentum first picked up in this sector, there was much anticipation that the investment tax credit promised by candidate Clinton would play a role in boosting or sustaining it, but the investment tax credit never materialized. Meanwhile, the surge in capital spending continued unabated.

> "No investment tax credit. No change in appreciation rules. No special deals of any kind aimed at capital investment. Yet the U.S. is enjoying a remarkable boom in business equipment investment both in the heavy machinery that runs the factory and in the lighter gear that makes the office go."
>
> Fortune, April 1995

As discussed earlier, in some cases it takes interest rates a while to gain traction. And such was the case with business investments in equipment, but rates did begin to have an impact in 1992 and that momentum continued into the years following. By December 1992 industry watchers were anticipating a boom in capital equipment expenditures based on the favorable performance of this sector over the course of the year. And, their predictions were right on.

By now the powerful impact of low interest rates should be self evident. First mortgage refinancing caught fire, then home construction and sales, then the home improvement industry, then business investment in capital equipment and so on. Each additional market that ignited fueled the others by stimulating spending, generating business profits, creating jobs, boosting consumer confidence, i.e., all of the elements required to produce a vibrant economy. Before long every aspect of the economy was benefitting from the spark provided by interest rates.

The Missing Connection between Interest Rates and Clinton Administration Policy

There were two major waves of mortgage refinancing during the '90s and both were triggered by historically low interest rates. As we have shown, construction was also a beneficiary of low interest rates. If Clinton administration policies were responsible for driving interest rates lower, then the administration should be credited for the economic benefit that accrued. The evidence we've considered so far suggests otherwise. However, this critically important question is worth a more in-depth look.

The Clinton Administration was well aware of the importance of interest rates to the success of the economy, and shortly after taking office Bill Clinton began to claim that his policies had helped reduce interest rates by 100 basis points. A number of experts also joined the bandwagon proclaiming that Clinton's policies had begun to benefit the economy even before they had been passed by Congress. As early as one month into his administration, some economists were pointing to Clinton's promise of deficit reduction as the reason why interest rates were declining, in the process ignoring the fact that key interest rates had already declined substantially in the previous year well before Clinton had been elected.

In fact, during George H. W. Bush's (Bush 41) administration interest rates decreased by 610 basis points, including 111 basis points in 1992 alone[173]. Clinton was clearly the beneficiary of those interest reductions though it is doubtful that he would credit Bush's policies for the substantial interest rate reductions that occurred during his administration. What's more, in the 12 years preceding the Clinton administration, interest rates had declined an average of 70 basis points a year, which is about the same amount they declined during the first year of Clinton's presidency[174].

In other words, administration policy didn't do anything extraordinary for interest rates at the outset of the Clinton era. At best they continued the pattern that had already been established by the previous two administrations. This may be a bit hard for some to swallow as Bush 41's failure to get reelected largely revolved around his handling of the economy. In retrospect, when facts are taken into account, he may not have done as bad a job as was previously thought. As the saying goes, "Hindsight is 20/20." By the way, it turns out that by the middle of '94 when Clinton had been in office a little over a year, interest rates were up again and the activity had begun to cool off.

The reason interest rates were such a powerful economic stimulus in 1993 and later on in the '90s was not simply that they declined but because they had hit a key inflection point, where the benefits of refinancing mortgages outweighed the costs for a large pool of homeowners and where home ownership became affordable to a large number of families who were previously shut out of the market because of cost. The rate reductions during the Reagan-Bush years positioned interest rates to hit this critical point. What's more, once rates hit this threshold and moved further below, the housing sector achieved enough elasticity so that even when rates edged up a bit, that movement dampened the momentum of the market but didn't kill it.

For example, when the average interest rate for 30-year fixed mortgages dipped into the low eights in '92, about a third of outstanding mortgages or around 6 million had rates of 10% or higher[175]. In contrast, 1.5 million homes or a quarter as many were refinanced in '91. Though the numbers in '91 were considered to be pretty strong, they were not strong enough to stimulate the broader economy. The value of mortgages refinanced in 1990 was less than half the total for 1991.

Meanwhile, as interest rates dipped, housing afford-ability jumped. In the fourth quarter of 1992, the National Association of Realtors (NAR) housing affordability index was measured at 129.6, up from 120.2 during fourth quarter of 1991, almost a full 10 points. This was the highest it had been since 1974, before interest rates got out of control in the mid-seventies[176].

The affordability index measures the ability of families earning the median income to buy a median-priced home. At a reading of 100, a median income family has exactly enough to buy a median-priced home with a conventional loan and a 20% down payment. At a reading of 129.6, a median income family has more than enough to purchase a median-priced home. Put another way more than half the families in the country could afford to buy a home. Once this critical point was achieved the stage was set for new buyers to enter the market in sizeable numbers. If for some reason it was not sustained, i.e., interest rates edged upward they would not. To use a weather analogy, this was the equivalent of having a storm warning versus a storm watch; conditions were set and a home buying spree was on the way. It was only a matter of time. Unlike weather though, there were moves the new administration could make that would kill the energy, but there really wasn't anything it needed to do kick off the buying.

What about the low interest rates that set off the second wave of refinancing in late '97? What was the driver behind them? With respect to the housing sector activity in the latter part of the '90s, there is widespread agreement that interest rate reductions were largely due to the Asian financial crisis. After, currency devaluations and meltdowns in financial markets in Thailand, Malaysia and Indonesia during summer of '97, there was a mass exodus out of Asian securities and into US financial markets, which drove a dramatic decline in long-term interest rates. By mid-1998 foreigners owned nearly 40 percent of the privately held federal debt, which is double the rate of foreign ownership in 1994[177].

The Asian-induced decline of long-term interest rates became a catalyst for a whole chain of interrelated economic activity including lower mortgage rates, higher housing demand, increased sales of household appliances and furnishings and, of course, a torrid pace of mortgage refinancing. The Clinton Administration could not be blamed for the Asian financial crisis and neither can it take credit for the economic benefit that it generated.

In the interest of completeness, it is important to point out that there were some negative aspects of the Asian crisis relative to the US economy, including larger trade deficits, stock market dips and more. In fact, a number of economists were of the opinion that the crisis would have a net negative effect on the economy. However, what transpired here highlights the benefit of being in the midst of an economic perfect storm as we've suggested was the case at the time, i.e., that when one of the contributing factors slows down, another one picks up so there is no loss of overall momentum. It turns out that the net negative impact of the Asian crisis that was expected by economists never materialized.

One thing is clear. There was widespread agreement that the impact of low interest rates or "cheap money" was greater than any economic stimulus proposed or enacted by the President. The administration itself claimed that a one percent reduction in long-term interest rates equated to $100 billion in economic stimulus. Meanwhile, according to the Washington Post, industry models constructed by renowned firms like DRI/McGraw Hill put the figure as low as $30 billion or as high as $70 billion[178]. Economist Michael Evans estimated that a 1 percentage point drop in long-term rates would equate to $60 billion in added goods and services and up to 400,000 additional jobs[179].

In this case, theory squares with reality when we consider what transpired in mortgage refinancing, housing construction and sales, and CAPEX during the '90s as well as their impact on the economy. By itself, cheap money was a powerful economic stimulus and jobs creator. When combined with the other four factors that were in play at the time, it is not much of a leap in reasoning to conclude that the US was truly in the midst of something unique: an economic perfect storm. When investigated as to its drivers it's not much of a leap to conclude that the administration didn't have much to do with the emergence of this force.

Chapter 6: Large pool of unsophisticated investors

ᘛ ᘚ

A nother major driver of the historic economic expansion of the '90s was the influx of record numbers of first-time or unsophisticated investors into the securities markets. This phenomenon is closely related to the Internet boom and the impact of the Telecom Act of 1996; they created the buzz that drew investors into the market. However, the magnitude of the impact of this economic driver requires that it be dealt with separately. According to the Federal Reserve, between 1991 and 1997, U.S. household assets grew by $11 trillion and about 60 percent of that growth was due to ownership of stocks or shares in mutual funds or pensions invested in stocks. Direct stock ownership alone produced 25 percent of U.S. household wealth in the 1990s versus a mere 5 percent in the 1970s and 9 percent in the 1980s[180].

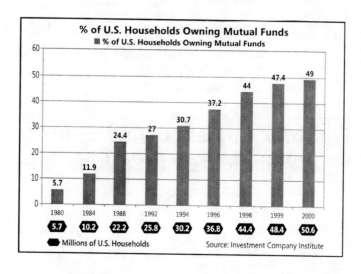

% of U.S. Households Owning Mutual Funds

Source: Investment Company Institute

At the beginning of the 1990s about 25 percent of US households owned mutual funds; however, by 2000 the percentage of households with ownership in mutual funds had risen to nearly 50 percent according to the Investment Company Institute[181]. In 1990 there were 23 million mutual fund accounts, but by 1998 there were already 100 million mutual fund accounts[182]. In just one year, from 1999 — 2000, five million Americans became mutual fund shareholders for the first time[183]. Over the course of the 1990s and into the first year of the new millennium more than 30 million Americans became shareholders for the first time[184].

The influx of first time investors into the market is significant because unsophisticated investors behave in fundamentally differently ways than seasoned investors. Seasoned investors are familiar with the ups and downs of the market. They know that no matter how long a run up in the market continues; sooner or later there will be a downturn. Investors who become shareholders for the first time during a bull market are only familiar with the market's movement in an upward direction and are more susceptible to thinking that it will always be that way. This can lead to irrational and even unprofitable behaviors. For example, even though stock prices may be completely out of synch with the fundamentals typically used to determine them, unsophisticated investors are willing to pay those prices because of the belief they will continue rising ever higher, which in turn will provide them with an opportunity to make a profit.

These are exactly the conditions that existed during the bull market of the late 1990s. Historically, stocks had sold for at anywhere from around 10 to 30 times their current year earnings per share, but many Internet stocks were trading at hundreds of times their earnings; yet, investors were still buying. Some notable examples include Yahoo, which traded at more than 300 times its projected earnings for 1998[185] and Amazon, whose stock price rose from $13 a share to $221 a share in one year despite the fact that it was losing money at the time[186]. Overall, in 1999, Nasdaq stocks, which had historically traded at 20 to 40 times earnings, had a composite price to earnings ratio of over 100[187]. These conditions raised red flags for many Wall Street veterans who in turn sounded alarms that disaster was impending, but their warnings fell on deaf ears of unsophisticated investors who were driven more by a lottery mentality than by a well-researched approach to investing.

"When sanity returns valuations will plummet laying waste to the millions of unsophisticated investors who bought Net stocks without questioning their true worth."[188]

Michael Murphy
California Technology Stock Letter
May, 1999

"Look at the high-yield (junk bond) market in the mid-'80s. Go back to the late-'70s and early '80s commodities cycle. It's the same type of action: The market chugs along, starts to catch people's interest, then you get a herd effect. There's excessive speculation, then purging and then the penalty phase — when the wave of euphoria turns to a wave of gloom."[189]

Michael Clark
CS First Boston
September, 1998

Investors' behavior at the time could be compared to that of people lining up to buy a lottery ticket when the jackpot has reached astronomical proportions. Even people with the most conservative views about gambling have been known to purchase a lottery ticket or two during these times even though the chance of winning anything is slim to none. How much more would people with some spare cash on hand be inclined to try their hand at investing in stocks in an environment where a Wall Street veteran like James Grant (Editor, Grant's Interest Rate Observer) described a share of stock as "no longer anything so humble as a mere claim on the discounted future earnings of a business, but rather a lottery ticket with a near certain payoff."[190]

New investors were driven more by stories of how relatives' and friends' modest investments in Internet and Telecom companies had made them independently wealthy overnight than by time honored principles of investing. There was no shortage of such stories once the Internet boom and the resulting IPO frenzy kicked into high gear. Of course there were the stories of college kids founding Internet companies, taking them public and becoming mega millionaires or billionaires overnight. Among these were people like Jerry Yang and David Filo of Yahoo whose stakes were valued at $132 million a piece when the company went public in 1996[191] or Todd Krizelman and Stephan Paternot of theglobe.com whose stakes were valued at $35M a piece when the company went public in fall of 1998[192]. But nothing captured the fancy of the public like supermarket clerks with six-figure 401Ks or the person next door that hit it big with a stock pick and was able to buy a car or vacation home cash down.

A poll by Newsweek taken in 1999[193] showed that almost half of all people who earned $50,000 or more knew someone who had become rich. Meanwhile, it also showed that 67 percent of Americans who earned $30,000 to $49,000 felt that they had missed out on the Internet boom. There was no shortage of sentiment within the ranks of middle class that they were missing out or that they had missed out on their chance to achieve a measure of financial independence. These feelings were reinforced by ads being run by online brokerage firms depicting the likes of a tow truck driver becoming rich enough off his investments to buy himself an island or a teen making enough off online trading to buy himself a helicopter.

It's not surprising that when the opportunity presented itself these people got involved in the market. That in itself was not a problem, but there were some other surrounding factors that were. For one thing, many first timers entered the market when it was already grossly overvalued so they were already operating at a disadvantage. Their chances of coming out on the positive side of the ledger were slim. Meanwhile, the influx of funds from new entrants came mainly in the form of mutual fund investments, which created a large pool of capital that fund managers were obligated to invest. These dollars helped to circumvent normal correction cycles of the market giving the impression that the market could overcome any kind of adversity and continue its upward climb. This combined with pronouncements by high flying analysts that the Internet had ushered in a new economic order lulled newcomers into a false sense of security causing them to ignore warning signs that a major downturn was on the horizon.

Another thing is that new entrants were not content to settle for what amounted to healthy returns by historical standards. Their expectations had been raised by the spectacular returns others had enjoyed. It wasn't just about what they could make. It was about what they could have made. As a result, when the market finally started to retreat toward levels that were more consistent with the financials of publicly traded companies, many of these folks held on to their investments too long. One expert quoted in Saturday Night summed it up this way:

> "And then the unsophisticated investors invest because they think it's easy money and then they're left holding an empty bag. The dumb money always gets in last and leaves last"[194]

> Jim Rodgers
> Chair of the Canadian Association of
> Insurance and Financial Advisers
> February, 2001

Studies by a variety of academics have identified counterproductive behaviors that tend to be more pronounced in inexperienced investors, including the following:[195]

- Taking unusual investment risks simply for fear of losing out. In the words of Thomas Gilovich, a Cornell psychology professor, "If you don't take the chance, you'll feel that you've fallen behind."
- Holding on to losers too long and selling winners too early
- Assuming that direct control of trading one's portfolio will make it possible to avoid losses

- Attributing limited success in the market (e.g., one or two successful stock purchases) to one's own investment prowess

A study conducted by Paine Webber, the Gallup Organization, and the Wall Street journal provided empirical evidence that novice investors in the bull market tended to be more optimistic than seasoned investors. On practically every measure of optimism, new investors were more optimistic. For example, even though industry experts were sounding the alarm that returns from 1995 through 1998 were unsustainably high, only 39% of investors with five years or less in the market felt that the market was overvalued compared with 58% of investors with 21 or more years in the market. When asked about what type of return they expected in the following year, novice investors expected an 18% return while seasoned investors expected a return in the neighborhood of 14%. Meanwhile, Wall Street analysts considered a normal return to be around 10% or less. Even when asked about their returns for the previous 12 months novice investors painted a more positive picture. They reported average returns of 19% while participants in the study overall reported returns of 16.9%[196].

The stock market run up was rooted more in market psychology than in any kind of economic fundamentals. In fact, there are characteristics of the 1990s market boom that were eerily similar to conditions that existed just prior to the infamous crash of 1929 that ushered in the Great Depression, and what do you know, the crash that followed the 1990s boom had many similarities to the 1929 crash as well. A New York Times article by Ron Chernow (author of Titan: The Life of John D. Rockefeller Sr.) published in 1998 identified several similarities between the period leading up to the crash in 1929 and the period leading to the crash in 1997, which after all turned out to be a preview of a much bigger "coming contraction."

One similarity between these periods is that the stock market became ubiquitous in the popular culture. Instead of a passing mention at the end of the evening news, coverage of the stock market became front and center on all of the major network evening news programs. Cable television channels sprang up to keep the public informed of what was going on in the markets, and the anchors on these channels became as recognizable as personalities on popular television shows. Newsweek related story of Sue Herera who realized just how many people were tuning in to watch her show when a truck driver yelled out to her, "Hey Sue, where's the Dow going?" In the same article a Boston stockbroker is quoted as saying "Now I feel like a rock star" whereas in previous years her experience at parties was that people "used to run to the other end of the room" when she revealed her profession[197].

Another similarity between the periods leading up to the crashes of 1929 and 1997 is the entry of the "little people" on to the financial stage, i.e., people who are not in the position to lose the money invested in the market without it affecting their lifestyle. For the most part, investing in the stock market has been the domain of affluent families who can afford to lose their entire investment without affecting their lifestyle. However, during periods when the market appears to be a "can't miss" opportunity with easy money to be made, it attracts participation by people from all walks of life. These also tend to be periods of high speculation, when the market is driven more by emotion than economic fundamentals making it more risky for all participants.

Historically, large scale participation by people at the lower end of the income spectrum has occurred just before a major plunge. One of the most well known stories that illustrates this concept is the account of Joe Kennedy (father of John F., Bobby, Teddy, et. al.) who decided to get out of the market in 1929 after receiving a stock tip from his shoeshine man. The crash occurred shortly thereafter[198]. Similar phenomenon, though not quite as dramatic, occurred with the Nifty Fifty in the late '60s to early '70s, commodities markets in the late '70s to early '80s and the junk bond market in the mid-'80s. The late 1990s continued the pattern as truckers, cab drivers, garage attendants, and others atypical of the Wall Street investment crowd got involved. By the end of the '90s more than half of investors in the stock market had incomes less than $50,000 annually[199].

A third similarity between the pre-crash periods was assurances from analysts that a new economic order had been ushered in that would be free from market corrections, business cycles, and bear markets. During the 1920's there was a belief that as a result of the creation of the Federal Reserve System the market would be kept safe from crashes. During the 1990's a similar mantra was being chanted. Though many stock valuations seemed to be insane when compared against time honored pricing methodologies, investors were continually assured that as a result of the "e" revolution, the rules had changed and these valuations made sense. And, the market cooperated too surging ahead for seven straight years without a single 10 percent correction even though these had typically occurred at two- to three-year intervals.

Despite the similarities to the pre-Depression period, the influx of cash into the market was legendary. Early in 1998 capital was flowing into stock mutual funds at a rate of $21 billion a month[200]. In February of 2000 over $50 billion was channeled into the stock mutual funds in just one month[201].

Several factors played a role in unsophisticated investors' participation in the market. For example, one by-product of the Web revolution was that market statistics, which were once the domain of financial insiders, became readily available to the general public, and the public consumed them voraciously. At one point AOL members were requesting 70 million stock quotes per day[202]. A whole group of websites sprang up that were specifically devoted to providing market statistics, investment research and stock tips, including www.fool.com and www.thestreet.com not to mention a whole collection of sites that enabled people to place their own trades like www.ameritrade.com, www.etrade.com and, www.schwab.com. In concert with the web resources, new cable networks were launched like Bloomberg Television, CNBC and CNNFn to focus primarily on covering financial markets. There were also a number of new magazines that hit the newsstands, which were devoted to investment information and education, e.g., Smart Money and Worth.

Resources like these are so embedded in the mainstream culture now that it is hard to fathom that before the mid-nineties none of them existed. As a result of them, some key barriers to market entry were removed: 1) basic market education, 2) access to securities pricing information, 3) high cost of participation reflected in traditional brokerage fees, 4) ease of executing a securities trade, and 5) ability to exercise direct control over one's portfolio.

There were also other phenomena that aided unsophisticated investors' participation in financial markets. The 1990s were characterized by unprecedented growth in investment phenomenon such as investment clubs and day trading. For example, according to the National Association of Investors Corp., in 1997 membership in investment clubs stood at 550,000, which is five times the number of members in 1986[203].

Day traders are investors who hope to profit from minute by minute fluctuation in stock prices. Armed with analytics and technology for executing instantaneous trades, which were made easily accessible by the web revolution, this new breed of investor bucked the norms of classic Wall Street investing. They adopted a model of making dozens of trades per day and cashing out all of their stock positions by the market close. The idea was to make small profits on each transaction, which would add up to a substantial amount of money when multiplied by the number of transactions.

Estimates of how many people were involved in day trading range from a few thousand to tens of thousands. It is known that around 100 companies were set up to service day traders, some with as many as 1,500 patrons[204]. These companies provided infrastructure to support traders, including techniques purported to minimize risk, training/mentoring to develop trading expertise, and trading capital provided either on a shared risk basis or as direct loans. Research shows that only a small percentage of day traders made money even at the height of bull market. Nevertheless, the practice attracted thousands from all walks of life who quit their steady jobs to become traders. According to the North American Securities Administrators Association Inc. the people they found at day trading companies were "unsophisticated investors lured into the practice of day trading by talk of hefty gains and minimal risks."[205]

The ranks of the investor pool were also buoyed by the numbers of baby boomers who were reaching the age where funding retirement became an important consideration. One industry expert, Harry Dent, was so convinced of the impact of this demographic on the market's dynamics that he predicted the Dow would reach 35,000 by 2009. Lest you write him off as a quack you should know that in 1989 he had also predicted that the Dow would reach 10,000 despite the fact that a luminary like Alan Greenspan had previously said that a Dow average of 6,000 was unattainable[206]. Other experts also cited the baby boomer demographic as a key driver of the bull market. John Wyatt put it this way in a Fortune magazine article that came out right around the time the market began to take off:

"But it's not Wall Street or even Silicon Valley that's driving the latest IPO boom. It's you. Stoked by the retirement anxieties of baby-boomers, investors poured a staggering $71.4 billion of new cash into equity mutual funds in the first quarter alone-blowing the doors off the previous record. Mutual fund managers, the biggest buyers of IPOs, are pressed to put the money to work quickly, and to get results"[207]

However, perhaps the most important factor that stimulated first time investors' participation in the stock market was the epic shift from employer funded pension plans (a.k.a. defined benefit plans) to joint employer-employee funded retirement plans (a.k.a. 401(k) or defined contribution plans). 401(k) plans began to rise in popularity during the 1980s as a result of five key factors: 1) legislation that increased restrictions on defined benefit plans, 2) employers' need to control pension costs, 3) competitive pressures to offer attractive benefit plans, 4) employees' desire for greater portability in pension plans, and 5) employers' desire to add retirement options to their benefit packages.

On the strength of these factors, from 1984 to 1993 the proportion of companies offering 401(k) plans increased from 34 percent to 60 percent[208]. In raw numbers, from 1984 to 1995 the number of companies offering 401(k)s increased from 436,000 to 660,000. Meanwhile, over the same period the number of defined benefit plans offered by employers decreased from 168,000 to 78,000[209]. By 1995, more stocks were owned by defined contribution retirement plans than the sum total of those owned by all traditional US pension funds[210].

In response to aggressive promotion of the plans by employers, participation rates also increased dramatically. By 1994 more than 40 million Americans were enrolled in 401(k) plans versus a negligible amount just 15 years earlier[211]. By 1998 80 percent[212] of those eligible to participate in plans were enrolled versus 68 percent[213] in 1990. Once companies took the step of incorporating 401(k) plans into their portfolio of benefits, they also took steps to educate employees about the availability of the plans as well as about how the plans needed to be managed in order to obtain a suitable benefit upon retirement. By 1993 three quarters[214] of employers were offering some type of investment education for employees and by 1996 eighty-six percent[215] offered such education. Also by the end of the nineties many employers had implemented automatic enrollment 401(k) plans, which also had the effect of increasing plan participation and in turn stock market participation. By 2000 around half of American households were stockholders versus one third in 1989[216]. This is a huge amount of statistics to digest all at once, but they all boil down to one thing, which is succinctly expressed by one industry insider in the following quote:

"You've got hundreds of billions of dollars being handed over to tens of millions of first-time investors."[217]

Michael J. Francis
Vice President
Smith Barney Shearson Inc.

As a result of these changes in the pension landscape, millions of Americans got their first taste of the stock market through the funds included in their 401k plans. This shift also thrust average Americans into the unfamiliar role of managing their own retirement funds, a role that had previously been filled by seasoned investment professionals who managed institutional pension funds, who, by the way, behave quite differently than the newbies. So not only did millions of Americans suddenly find themselves as stockholders for the first time, they also had to watch the market and make decisions about what to buy and sell. The net effect of this was that novice investors were put in the position of exerting unprecedented influence in the equities markets. Throw in a dose of unprecedented accessibility to market information, the ability to execute transactions in near real time plus some good ole upward market momentum, and you have a recipe for a stock market bubble.

These plans also became another source of cash for the public as many employers offered employees the opportunity to borrow from their 401(k) for big ticket items like house down payments or college tuition. This provision was particularly appealing to plan participants because in effect they'd be borrowing from themselves versus taking out loans from a bank.

The market's run up during the nineties was nothing short of spectacular. It experienced a five-fold increase from 3 trillion to 15 trillion[218] and had a profound impact on the economy. Once again, having been in office at the time, the Clinton administration is positioned to take credit for the market's performance. However, without the pool of unsophisticated investors that existed at the time as well as the factors that aided their participation in stock ownership, the market probably would not have had a run like it did. What's more, the key pieces of legislation that prompted a shift in pension policies and helped to nudge this pool of investors into the market were passed in the 1980s:

- The Omnibus Budget Reconciliation act of 1987, which limited funding of defined benefit pension plans to 150 percent of plan termination liability, which includes only benefits accrued to date. Previously, plans could fund up to 100 percent of their projected liability[219].

- The Tax Reform Act of 1986, which reduced the maximum salary used to calculate future pension benefits-first from $235,000 to $200,000. The Omnibus Budget Reconciliation act of 1993, a Clinton era bill, subsequently further reduced this to $150,000[220].

From the evidence presented in this chapter, it would appear that factors like pension policies, access to market information and new investor psychology provide a much better explanation for the market's outstanding run than any kind of administration policy.

Chapter 7: PCs Set the Table and the Census tops it off

⌣: ⌤

Two other factors that played a role in stimulating the Clinton era economy ought to be mentioned: 1) the coming of age of the PC and 2) the decennial census. In a very real sense, PC technology set the table for the prosperity of the nineties. At its core the economic expansion revolved around a revolution in information technology. That revolution was launched by the arrival of the PC as well as the companies that had a hand in advancing the technology. The runaway success of companies like Apple, Compaq, Dell, Oracle and especially Microsoft primed investors to look for the next big opportunity. When it looked like it had arrived in the form of Internet companies like Netscape, they jumped on it. That's just one of the ways PCs had a hand in the growth economy.

At the other end of the spectrum is a seemingly insignificant event that is mandated by law: the decennial census. It happens every ten years and nobody pays much attention to the economic stimulus it delivers. However, when added to the cumulative effect of the other economic forces that were in play at the time, what would normally be an afterthought takes on added significance. One could say it topped off the steady stream of favorable economic conditions that characterized the period. The rest of this chapter adds additional details surrounding the contributions of PCs and the census to the nineties economy.

The PC was the paradigm shifting technology breakthrough that helped to drive the economic expansion of the eighties, but it also played a big role in driving the economy of the nineties. During the late '80s and early '90s headlines predicting the end of the PC boom were very common. And, the industry did experience a bit of a dip in the early '90s, but there were numerous factors that contributed to a revival of the industry from 1993 onward, including wave after wave of innovations in processor speed, multimedia technology, portability, operating systems (OS), and desktop applications. These innovations enabled end users to add ever increasing computing capabilities at lower and lower price points. Rapid introduction of faster and faster chips like the Pentium and the Pentium II drove price reductions. OS innovations like Windows 95, Windows NT and Window 2000 added capabilities like multitasking, enterprise grade network management capabilities, and Y2K readiness.

Meanwhile, some of the economic drivers that have already been discussed, Y2K, the Internet revolution and cheap money, also contributed to the phenomenal growth of the PC industry during the nineties. For example, given the dramatic decline in the cost of PCs as well as the additional functionality to be had, many companies found it simpler to prepare for Y2K by swapping out their stock of existing PCs and software applications for new ones rather than investing in remediation. In the meantime, it turned out that PCs and the Internet had a symbiotic relationship. The PC was instrumental in helping to pave the way for widespread usage of the Internet and the Internet in turn became a "killer application" for the PC. The emergence of the Internet as a mainstream communications medium introduced a whole new set of possibilities for how end users could use PCs and also provided end users with a whole new set of incentives to use them. The Internet revolution transformed the PC from a "nice to have" appliance to a "must have" productivity tool. As a result, whereas in the eighties PCs gained acceptance as part of the popular culture and families took the big step of buying the first PC for the home, in the nineties, the concept of adding PCs for multiple family members gained traction.

In addition to all of this, PC adoption in untapped (or barely tapped) global markets gained momentum, adding yet another catalyst to drive PC sales. For example, at the beginning of the 1990s in a technologically advanced country like Japan, only 2% of the population[221] were PC users so it's pretty clear that the worldwide upside potential for PCs during the nineties was enormous and U.S. manufacturers were major players.

The combination of all of these factors produced some extraordinary growth statistics for the PC industry during the nineties and along with them powerful economic stimulus. For example, an estimated 21 million PCs were sold worldwide in 1989, including 9 million in the U.S[222]. Meanwhile, in 1998 almost 93 million PCs were sold worldwide, including 36 million units in the U.S[223]. The industry enjoyed substantial year over year double digit growth for the better part of the nineties, at some points surging ahead by as much as 25 percent[224]. Specifically, unit sales of PCs grew by 13, 20, and 19 percent in 1996, 1997, and 1998[225]. In 1990 high-tech equipment (i.e., computers, communications gear, and instruments) represented 20 percent of all U.S. business investment, which includes everything from office buildings to industrial machinery. By 1998, its share of business investment had swelled to 40 percent[226]. In terms of domestic use, in 1990 PC penetration stood at approximately 15 percent, but by the end of the decade around 50 percent of U.S. homes owned a PC[227].

It's a bit challenging to separate out the economic impact of the PC industry growth versus the impact of economic drivers like Y2K, the Internet or cheap money because they are so closely intertwined. What we do know is that during the 1990s the computer industry gained more than one million jobs[228]. Trying to assign credit for the creation of these jobs presents us with the classic "Which one came first, the chicken or the egg?" problem. In other words, did PC-related innovations fuel the growth associated with Y2K, the Internet, and cheap money or did the stimulus provided by these other economic engines fuel PC purchases and in turn the job growth that resulted from that? It's hard to say.

However, it is safe to say that without the PC's widespread adoption as a mainstream business as well as household tool, the other economic drivers would not have been as potent as they were. Also, without the steady stream of innovations from bellwethers like Intel and Microsoft, PC industry growth would not have been as robust as it was and corresponding job growth would not have been as vibrant so the PC was an economic force in its own right. Finally, all of this came about as a result of private enterprise. Try as hard as we might, there isn't a government connection or more specifically a Clinton connection to be found here.

It was also fortuitous for President Clinton that the decennial census occurred on his watch and that it occurred right around the time when other economic catalysts were losing steam. For many people the mention of the decennial census in connection with the economy is almost certain to elicit a response along the lines of "Huh, what has the decennial census got to do with economic stimulus?" However, in the twilight of his presidency the census delivered Bill Clinton what he had sought to generate with an economic stimulus package that failed to pass Congress at the beginning of his tenure, i.e., 500,000[229] jobs distributed across the entire country. The timing of this boost was especially important because census hiring was ramping up just as Y2K was winding down, the Federal Reserve board was pulling liquidity out of the market, and Dot-coms were on the verge of collapsing. But for this statutory jobs program, the economic slowdown in 2000 might have been even more pronounced. Once again, due to no fault of its own the administration was positioned to enjoy the benefits of positive economic momentum. You could say that the decennial census was the cherry that topped off the economic bounty that ideal conditions delivered during Clinton's tenure.

Chapter 8: Summarizing the Economic Perfect Storm

ᴗ⦂ᴗ

The phrase "drinking from a fire hose" is sometimes used to describe how someone feels when he/she is presented with a lot of information in a compressed time frame. And, given how much information has been covered about the nineties economy in the preceding chapters, there's a good chance that you can identify with the "fire hose" feeling at this point. Now would be a good time to pause and summarize the high points from our discussion of the components of the economic perfect storm.

The book started off with a hypothesis that the prosperity of the nineties was driven by five forces that came together to form an economic perfect storm. The preceding chapters have shown how each one of these forces contributed to the vitality of the economy during that era and have examined to what extent the Clinton administration did or did not have a part in setting these forces in motion or contributing to their momentum. The case in favor of these elements as the center-piece of the Booming Nineties is quite strong. Meanwhile, the administration's minimal contribution in these areas is striking. Below is a table that presents a synopsis of each of the economic drivers, what was its impact, who or what were the movers and shakers that played a role in its potency as a catalyst for economic growth as well as an estimate of the Clinton administration's contribution to the impact of that driver.

Economic Driver	Economic Impact	Movers & Shakers	Clinton Contribution
Y2K	• Unleashed $100-$200 billion of IT spending • Unleashed emergency preparedness spending • Created 500k plus jobs • Exacerbated IT labor shortage • Stimulated salary growth	• Peter de Jager • Representative Steve Horn • Representative Tom Davis • Representative Constance Morella • Big Six Accounting Firms • Howard Rubin	■ Clinton ▨ Shakers
World Wide Web / Web Browser	• Generated $1.7 trillion in revenue • Created 3.1 million plus jobs • Stimulated salary growth • Fueled IPO Frenzy • Venture capital • Hiked real estate prices • Exacerbated IT Labor shortage	• Tim Berners Lee • Marc Andreesen • Eric Bina • Jim Clark (Netscape co-founder)	■ Clinton ▨ Shakers

Economic Driver	Economic Impact	Movers & Shakers	Clinton Contribution
Telecom Act of 1996	• $150 billion in capital expenditures • 352k jobs • Exacerbated IT labor shortage • Stimulated salary growth	• Big Three Long distance carriers • Baby bells • Republican congressional leaders • European Union • Senator Ernest Hollings • Senator John Danforth • Senator Bob Kerrey	■ Clinton ▦ Shakers
Cheap Money	• Unleashed $74 - $150 billion into economy • Triggered refinancing booms in '92-'94 and '97-'98 • Stimulated housing starts • Increased housing affordability • Boosted capital equipment spending	• Federal reserve board • Homeowners • Asian financial crisis • Reagan – Bush policy • The Omnibus Budget Reconciliation act of 1993	■ Clinton ▦ Shakers
Unsophisticated Investors	• Fueled five-fold increase in stock market from $3 trillion to $15 trillion • Supported $11 trillion increase in household assets	• Individual investors • Fund managers • Online brokerages • Investment clubs • Day traders • Shift from defined benefit to defined contribution retirement plans • Start-up international capital markets	■ Clinton ▦ Shakers

One other important item needs to be summarized, and that is how many jobs were generated by these economic forces considering that the Clinton boast of 22 million jobs created is one of the central claims that is under scrutiny in this book. This is a challenging proposition because several of the drivers are closely related. As a result, it is hard to tally the jobs they generated without some amount of double counting. That said, more than enough information has been pulled together to take a credible stab at it.

The following table provides a roll-up of the jobs that were created by the "Fab Five" economic drivers. The figures in this table are derived from jobs data provided in other parts of the book. Wherever there is a range of possibilities for a jobs estimate, the roll-up errs toward the low side of the range to guard against overstating the case. For example, earlier in the book when the job multiplier effect was discussed, it was shown that for each Internet economy or TA-96 job created as many as seven additional jobs were created, but the roll-up uses a multiplier of two. Even so the result is still stunning.

Also, in one case jobs data linked to one driver in the narrative is reflected in the roll-up in connection with another driver, i.e., jobs data for IPOs and Venture Capital was spelled out in the chapter on the Internet revolution, but for purposes of the roll-up they are reflected under Unsophisticated Investors. As a matter of fact, because of the close relationship between these two drivers, the IPO and VC jobs data could have easily been presented in either chapter. The key thing is that in the roll-up these jobs are only counted once.

Economic Driver	Cash Infusion	Direct Jobs Created	Multiplier Jobs	Jobs Total
Y2K	$100 - $200 billion	.3 - .7 million*	1.5 million	2.0 million
Worldwide Web	$1678 billion	3.1 million	6.0 million	9.1 million
Telecom Act of 1996	$150 billion	.4 million	1.1 million	1.5 million
Cheap Money	$74 - $154 billion	2.0 million	----	2.0 million
Unsophisticated Investors	$11 - $12 trillion	2.1 million	--	2.1 million
PC Comes of Age	--	1.0 million	2.0 million	**
Decennial census	--	.5 million	--	.5 million
Total	$13.0 - $14.2 trillion	8.6 million	8.6 million	17.2 million

*Midpoint of range used for calculations
**PC related jobs are not counted in the totals to avoid double counting

From the tally in this table, it is reasonably clear that without the boost provided by factors devoid of Bill Clinton's influence his performance on jobs creation would not be nearly as stellar as it is made out to be. More than three quarters of job growth of the period can be attributed to forces unrelated to the administration. The takeaway from these two tables is that the best explanation for the extraordinary prosperity of the nineties is an economic perfect storm. In other words, the Clinton economic boom is a myth.

Chapter 9: Myth Two - The Clinton Balanced Budget

꒤꒰

...Finally, balance the budget in 10 years. It took decades to run up this deficit; it's going to take a decade to wipe it out. Now mind you, we could do it in 7 years, as congressional leaders propose. But the pain we'd inflict on our elderly, our students, and our economy just isn't worth it.[230]

> William Jefferson Clinton
> Address from the Oval Office
> June 19, 1995

One of the accomplishments that Bill Clinton is most proud of is the fact that when he left office the Federal budget had been balanced and better still, budget surpluses were projected several years out. Everyone agrees that Clinton left office with a more favorable situation with respect to the federal budget than when he took office, but how did the balanced budget and the budget surpluses come about? Was it due to a master plan put in place by the president or once again was it due to factors that were not primarily driven by the president?

As a matter of fact President Clinton did make deficit reduction a priority when he first took office. The budget submitted by the White House for fiscal 1993 scaled back spending and increased taxes in an effort to get the deficit under control. As a candidate, Clinton had promised to balance the budget in five years. However, by the time he unveiled his third budget, Clinton's rhetoric about balancing the budget had changed. Even though his budgets contained smaller deficits than his predecessors, he was projecting deficits in the $150 - $200 billion range for several years out and did not consider it to be a problem.[231] Many observers felt that he had abandoned his stance on balancing the budget as is indicated by following sound bites from the media:

> "No one watching him back then — particularly among his friends — imagined that he had the slightest intention of balancing the budget, much less paying down the national debt." [232]

> Steve Chapman
> Editorial Board — Chicago Tribune
> January, 2001

> "Last week he told radio reporters that he favored a balanced budget in 10 years — a stance that surprised his assistants who had been stating a different position for months"[233]

> U. S. News & World Report
> June, 1995

"Last week, President Clinton experienced a conversion on the road to re-election by embracing a vision of a balanced budget."[234]

Alan Abelson
Barron's
June, 1995

"Faced with overwhelming pressure from the GOP majority in Congress and a dramatic shift in public opinion, President Clinton quit fighting on June 13, 1995. In his 6-minute prime-time speech, he joined the budget balancing crowd..."[235]

Howard Gleckman
Business Week
June, 1995

"Almost no one on Capitol Hill thinks the President is convinced of the economic or fiscal need for a balanced budget. Almost everyone thinks he suddenly produced a plan to balance the budget in 10 years because he thought it was in his own political interest."[236]

Adam Clymer
The New York Times
June, 1995

It was the Republican controlled Congress that got the President refocused on balancing the budget. Under pressure from Republicans who had first advocated a balanced budget amendment and later a plan to balance the budget in seven years, the President proposed a plan to balance the budget in 10 years. That was in 1995. In other words, the

Clinton plan would not have produced a balanced budget until 2005. Meanwhile, Mr. Clinton repeatedly referred to the Republican seven-year timetable in negative terms such as reckless, irresponsible or too painful.

> "The White House long has argued that seven years is simply too short a time to bring the budget into balance because it would mean Draconian cuts to programs serving the poor, elderly and disabled. They have argued instead for a nine-year plan."[237]

Hilary Stout and David Rogers
Wall Street Journal
October, 1995

> "The haste of their schedule and the scope of their tax cut are luxuries and this is not a time for luxuries," Mr. Clinton said."[238]

Alison Mitchell
New York Times
July, 1995

To cement his position, the President actually unveiled a plan to balance the budget in 10 years, but there was widespread agreement that his plan in fact did not accomplish this goal. The Congressional Budget Office, which Clinton had designated the final arbiter of budget numbers in his first State of the Union address, evaluated his plan and found that it would produce higher deficits than the 1995 level for every year of the plan, including a $209 billion deficit in the tenth year.

President Clinton and the Republican Congress eventually agreed on a plan to balance the budget by 2002, but only after a long and bitter battle characterized by stalemates and government shutdowns. This plan was passed into law as the Balanced Budget Act of 1997. During the budget standoff Republicans were unwavering about achieving the goal of a balanced budget and in the shortest possible time. Meanwhile, the President emphasized gradual deficit reduction and favored longer timetables to balance the budget, none of which would close the gap during his time in office. How then did we wind up with a balanced budget just a few years later? Was it due to flawless execution and over-achievement on the bipartisan budget plan?

In speeches and other public comments, President Clinton often points to the 1993 budget bill as the key driver for achieving a balanced budget during the latter part of the 1990s and applauds Democratic members of Congress for taking political risks to vote along with him on that bill. What many people do not realize is that the 1993 bill did not project to balance the budget. Instead, it projected that the deficit would decline from $255 billion in 1993 to $173 billion in 1996 then climb back up to about $200 billion in 1999[239]. The 1994 budget forecast even bigger deficits than the 1993 bill.

The deficit reduction measures instituted by the Clinton administration certainly contributed to closure of the budget gap. However, there is plenty of evidence to show that other factors were primarily responsible for balancing the budget and producing surpluses. In particular, several sources, including expert analyses presented in the Chicago Tribune, the Los Angeles Times and the Washington Post attribute the fiscal turnaround to a surge in tax revenues that stemmed from capital gains on booming mutual funds as well as tax liabilities for cashing stock options and larger salaries, all of which were primarily due to the Internet boom and the bull market fueled by it. In the late 1990s, these factors produced a string of unexpected windfalls, which surprised federal, state and local budget planners as tax revenues consistently came in above their estimates.

The California budget experience during this period is a microcosm of what happened at the national level and provides an excellent foundation for understanding the impact capital gains, stock options and higher salaries had on tax revenues. In April 1999 the Los Angeles Times reported that the California Finance Department had estimated that workers in the state had bolstered their pay by an additional $2 billion in the first quarter alone mainly through stock options but also through other bonuses as well. Just this stock option/bonus factor for one quarter translated into $200 million more in *personal income tax* revenue than the state was expecting. However, much of the windfall went back into the state's economy in the form of dollars spent on home remodeling, trips and other purchases, which would help to explain why during the first quarter of 1999 California *sales tax* revenue was also running at about $126 million above projections. When the billions that Californians realized during the first quarter from individual sales of stock are added into the mix, it is easy to see that the combination of capital gains, stock options and higher wages were critical factors in erasing deficits and creating surpluses.[240] In an article published May 7, 2000, the Los Angeles Times reported that California officials attributed the state's entire $9 billion windfall for 1999 to capital gains and stock option income.

To cement this idea, it is worthwhile to look at the impact of the trio in reverse, i.e., the impact on tax revenues from a sudden drop-off in capital gains and stock options. It turns out that just as the trio created unexpected windfalls in tax revenues during the stock market boom, when the Internet bubble burst and the equities markets crashed, the sharp falloff in capital gains created bigger than expected declines in tax receipts. For example, USA Today reported that in

California during the third quarter of fiscal 2001 workers' take-home pay declined by 6% instead of the 6% gain that was expected by budget planners. For the fiscal year overall, as a result of weak stock option and capital gains income, tax revenue declined by $6.6 billion instead of the $5.6 billion increase that was expected[241.]

The steep drop-off in options cashed by employees of just one of the leading California-based new economy companies sheds some light on this. During fiscal 2000, employees of Cisco Systems cashed in $7.1 billion worth of stock options, but in fiscal 2001 the value of stock options cashed by Cisco employees fell by 44% to $4 billion. Other states also felt the pinch of the drop-off in exercise of stock options, including Washington where options cashed in by Microsoft employees dropped by 63% to $5.9 billion and Oregon (the home of more Intel employees than any other state) where options exercised by Intel employees dropped by 73% to $486 million. To put this in perspective, in 1999 personal income in the state of Washington grew by 8%. Three percentage points of this increase were due solely to the stock options income of Microsoft employees. In USA Today, Changmook Sohn, the director of Washington's office of forecasting in 2001, is credited with commenting that stock options had been a "phenomenal contributor to the state's income" but that their role had been reversed[242].

The scenario that has just been described at the state level also played out at the national level on a grander scale. In just three years mutual funds capital gains, which are to a large extent stock market driven, went from producing 10% of all capital gains to producing nearly 20%. By the end of the 1990s capital gains had more than tripled. Meanwhile, between 1993 and 2000, the taxable income of the wealthiest 1.5% of all American grew by $600 billion, and their share of the tax burden grew from around 30% to more than

40%. These increases were mainly due to capital gains, stock options, and higher wages often driven by bonuses.[243]

The increases were also due in some part to changes to the tax code in 1990 and 1993, which generated some hefty tax bills for top earners to go along with their phenomenal income growth. According to the Los Angeles Times, nearly 60% of the tax windfall in the 1990s was drawn from less than 2% of the U.S. population. Contrary to popular belief it wasn't the middle class that benefited most from wage growth during the 1990s. Instead it was the wealthiest 1.5% of Americans. The $600 billion increase in their taxable income also represented half the country's total increase in disposable income.[244] Experts agree that it is precisely because so much of the 1990s income growth was concentrated at the top end of the income spectrum that the stock market boom translated into a tax revenue windfall; not a fact that the Clinton administration would like to advertise having positioned themselves as the advocates of the middle class.

An expert analysis presented in the May 7, 2000 edition of the Los Angeles times compares the total tax bill of 20 families with an income of $50,000 each versus the tax bill of one family of four with an income of $1,000,000. The total income in the two cases is the same, but under the tax code that was in place, the tax bills were very different: $13,000 (for 20 families) versus $361,000 (for 1 family). In the same piece a similar comparison at the state level revealed that the top 7.5% of income earners in the state of California took home 40% of the state's income and paid 66% of its taxes. Meanwhile, Californians with taxable incomes of $20,000 or less comprised more than 40% of the state's taxpayers but chipped in less than 1% of total income tax revenue.[245]

You can bet that it was not by design on the part of the Clinton administration that 86% of all income growth between 1990 and 1996 went to the top 20% of income earners[246]. This is the kind of thing President Clinton would accuse the Republicans of orchestrating. What's more, President Clinton's own comments (a few of which were cited earlier in the chapter) during the course of the rancorous budget battles of the 1990s show that he did not believe that budget could be balanced before the end of the decade without a significant amount of pain on the part of the average American.

However, during the 1990s there were some fundamental shifts in the allocation of assets for personal and institutional investments. According to the Federal Reserve, 24% of Americans' financial assets were in stocks or mutual funds in 1992. By 1998 this proportion had risen to 35% partially due to stocks' extraordinary gains but also due to more wide-spread ownership of stocks among American families[247]. This shift combined with the extraordinary, Internet inspired upswing in the stock market were critical factors in erasing the deficit and producing surpluses, which came about as a surprise to administration officials and Congress alike. The surprise factor was readily acknowledged by a variety of people in the know:

"For the past three years, April has been a great month for federal budget drafters, as waves of unexpected tax revenue made deficits sharply smaller or surpluses much bigger than anticipated."[248]

George Hager
Staff Writer - Washington Post
April 1999

"This is a tremendous opportunity and it is never going to come again in our lifetime. These kind of resources were unimaginable only five years ago"[249]

Jim Brulte
Chairman Senate Republican Caucus
January 2000

"During the late '90s, there was a series of favorable federal income tax surprises that pushed up revenues"[250]

John Youngdahl
Economist - Goldman Sachs
Los Angeles Times, April 2002

Even Al Gore didn't appear to recognize how much the government's fiscal health was dependent on the stock market or he might have tempered his comments about the surplus during the 2000 presidential campaign, considering that the stock market was already headed in the wrong direction.

The bottom line about the balanced budget and surpluses achieved at the end of the 1990s is that they were a surprise not the result of a carefully designed plan. President Clinton's comments on the subject during the early to mid-1990s show that he did not envision a balanced budget by the end of his administration or even for another several years beyond that. His fiscal policy had something to do with it, but the primary drivers were the Internet and TA-96 inspired stock market boom. In a nutshell, the Clinton balanced budget is a myth.

Chapter 10: Myth Three - Bill Clinton the Welfare Reformer

~:~

Whenever accomplishments of the Clinton administration are rattled off, invariably welfare reform is one of the topics that makes the list. Listening to Bill Clinton speak about welfare reform, one might think that he was the chief architect of the policy that eventually became law, i.e., that he articulated its principles, crafted it into a bill, built the consensus necessary to get it passed by Congress and subsequently signed it into law. There's no question that a fundamental shift in America's approach to welfare occurred during the Clinton years, but was it an administration-led initiative? Let's examine the evidence.

Candidate Clinton made welfare reform a central theme of his campaign strategy. It was the subject of ads he ran in swing states. In the ads and his stump speeches, he promised to change "welfare as we know it." However, despite the popularity of this issue with voters, it was months into his presidency before Clinton appointed a task force to define the administration's welfare reform policy and well into the second year of his administration before he submitted a welfare reform bill to Congress. Lo and behold, the long awaited Clinton bill did not pass!

From its perspective, the administration had good reason to delay action on welfare reform, but in so doing it lost control of the issue. The 1990s were unique in many ways and this even extended to the legislative arena. Normally the president defines the country's legislative agenda and negotiates with Congress to enact it. Following the mid-term elections of 1994 when the Republicans wrested control of both houses of Congress, there was a bit of a role reversal in this area. In an unprecedented move, Congressional leaders defined an extensive package of bills and proceeded to negotiate with the president to enact it. As a result, for a substantial portion of the Clinton administration, the legislative agenda was defined by Congress not the president, and the president was often relegated to providing input on someone else's bill instead of advancing one of his own. Some of the key accomplishments the administration cites are actually the result of this agenda and welfare reform was one of those.

Even before the 1994 elections, there was so much pent up demand for a welfare reform bill that no less than five bills were advanced by various members of Congress (partisan and bi-partisan)[251] prior to Clinton's failed offering. Within fourteen months of the 1994 elections, the Republican-led Congress passed two welfare reform bills, both of which were vetoed by the President. In the aftermath of the failed attempts to close the deal on welfare reform, the issue languished for a while. However, grass roots support on this subject was so strong that a number of states took the matter into their own hands and proposed or passed welfare reform bills at the state level, including Connecticut[252], Massachusetts,[253] Michigan,[254] Mississippi[255], and Wisconsin[256]. A federal bill was eventually signed by the President in August of 1996, more than three and a half years after he took office and just four months before the '96 Presidential elections.

Frankly, the bill that the President signed was not to his liking, but by this point another veto was politically untenable. The bill was skewed much more toward the Republican framework for welfare reform than the President's, and key Democrats who had initially supported the President's promise to deliver welfare reform were none too happy about that. For example, Daniel Patrick Moynihan who had initially been the President's chief Senate ally on welfare reform described the bill this way[257]

"The measure is not 'welfare reform,' it is 'welfare repeal.'"

However, on the strength of the ground swell of public support for action on the matter, this version of welfare reform was passed by substantial veto proof majorities in both houses (78 to 21 in the Senate and 328 to 101 in the House[258]) essentially making the President's signature on the bill irrelevant. Thus came about the historic transformation of the welfare system, hardly a Clinton led initiative. Put another way, Clinton led welfare reform is a myth.

Chapter 11: Selected Policy Issues Where Clinton Was "Out in Front"

꒰: ꒱

No matter what a president says about his policy priorities, what they actually are can be judged by the issues where he is willing to spend his political capital. These are the issues where he signs executive orders, submits bills to Congress, makes personal contacts with members of Congress to sway votes, and takes to the airwaves to sway public opinion. Throughout this book we have examined the involvement or lack of involvement of the Clinton administration in issues that had a major impact on the economic fortunes of the nineties. There were a number of policy initiatives where the administration was intensely engaged. The contrast between how these issues were handled by the administration versus the others is worth a short review to determine whether there is really a difference in the level of leadership President Clinton provided or if the analyses in previous chapters are unfairly denying him the credit he deserves. The following are some issues where Bill Clinton was on the front line.

- Healthcare Reform
- $16.3 Billion Economic Stimulus Package
- Reinventing Government / Fiscal Discipline

Healthcare Reform

Healthcare Reform is a great example of a policy issue where President Clinton clearly exercised leadership. For more than a year there was no mistaking that this was a priority of his administration. The President addressed a joint session of Congress on the topic and clearly spelled out the principles on which his healthcare reform initiative would be based. He submitted a detailed proposal to Congress as the basis of health-care reform legislation to the tune of 1300 plus pages[259].

The President was extremely vocal on the issue, making numerous public statements on the topic. Members of his cabinet were also advocates for the legislation. And, in an unprecedented move, the First Lady, Hilary Rodham-Clinton, was given a lead role in formulating the administration's proposal and was a leading spokesperson for the bill, second only to the President himself. The White House made frequent press releases on the subject and was constantly working with members of congress on provisions of the bill, e.g., employer mandates, subsidies for small businesses, the role of government in specifying the content of mandated health plans, caps on insurance premiums and so on.

As a result of the constant focus on it, healthcare reform even made it into the pop culture in the form of refer-ences on the "Tonight Show" as well as television ads. Yet, in December of 1994 the healthcare reform initiative was pronounced dead by Senate Majority Leader George Mitchell as Congress failed to come up with a version of legisla-tion that garnered the support of the public. Any number of reasons can be given for the failure of the initiative. Below are some of the top ones:

- The public perceived that under the provisions of the Clinton plan those who already had medical insurance would wind up paying more money while getting less choice.
- The public was uncomfortable with exchanging a market-based healthcare system for a government run system where federal bureaucrats would determine the coverage contained in healthcare plans and the premiums the public would pay

The administration's involvement in pushing healthcare reform provides a sharp contrast to its involvement in tackling issues like the Y2K problem or the telecommunications deregulation, both of which we have shown were pivotal to the nineties economy. For example, the President's public statements on the Y2K problem were few and far between plus they came late in the game after much prodding from members of Congress and industry experts when the outcome was pretty much decided.

The anticipated economic effects of the Clinton healthcare plan also contrast sharply with actual economic benefits delivered by Y2K and TA-96. For example, the White House had promoted healthcare reform as a deficit reducing measure and estimated that it would reduce the budget deficit by $60 billion[260] but the Congressional Budget Office estimated that it would add $70 billion[261] to the deficit. Analysis by independent experts agreed. A former chairman of the Council of Economic Advisors and economics professor at Harvard, Dr. Martin Feldstein, estimated that in 1997 alone the federal budget deficit would be 120 billion dollars more than the administration's estimate[262].

Also, the administration projected that insurance premiums would fall as a result of healthcare reform, but analysts estimated that 44% of Americans would pay more and among those some would pay as much as $1000 more[263].

The administration projected that healthcare reform would result in jobs growth, but analysts estimated that it could result in as many as two million jobs lost.

Given that Bill Clinton gets so much credit for skillfully managing the nineties economy, in some respects it's kind of ironic that a policy issue where Bill Clinton devoted so much time and exercised visible leadership was one that was projected to have negative economic impacts like lost jobs and larger budget deficits. One can't help but wonder if there ever would have been a federal budget surplus if Clinton's Health Security Act had passed. If that thought crossed your mind the following quotes suggest that you're not alone:

> "Many economists agree with Senator Daniel Patrick Moynihan, the chairman of the Senate Finance Committee, who says the Clinton system might run out of money; in that case, Congress would have to come to the rescue by raising taxes"[264]

> Time, February 14, 1994

> "The first flaw was that the act created a significant entitlement without establishing mechanisms to match the funding that would be available to the benefits promised."[265]

> Richard Clarke
> Columnist
> Healthcare Financial Management, November 1994

President Clinton is to be commended for taking on a problem as difficult as universal healthcare. After all 14 years later as the 2008 presidential elections are approaching, the problem still has not been solved. However, given the lessons learned perhaps a market-based approach would make the most sense for tackling the issue.

$16.3 Billion Economic Stimulus Package

About a month into his presidency Bill Clinton proposed a $16.3 billion economic stimulus package. It was designed to provide an immediate boost to the economy, which was still in the process of emerging from a recession. Among other things it contained the following:

- Extension of benefits for the long-term unemployed ($4 billion)
- Funding for highway projects ($3 billion)
- Funding for summer jobs for youths ($1 billion)

There was much debate about the package but it was never passed by Congress mainly for two reasons. First, the economy was showing signs of improving on its own. Second, the package would have increased the budget deficit for fiscal year 1993, and at a time when deficit reduction was a top priority on everyone's agenda it was difficult to justify any appropriation that would increase the deficit unless absolutely necessary.

Like healthcare reform, the economic stimulus package was clearly a priority for the President. The package was carefully crafted by the White House and submitted to Congress for action. It easily passed the House but encountered a stiff challenge in the Senate. In the face of opposition, Clinton worked tirelessly to get the package passed. When it encountered opposition from Senate Republicans, who filibustered the measure, the President offered a variety of compromise proposals scaling it back from its original price tag of $19.5 billion to $16.3 billion and finally to $12.2 billion[266]. He capitalized on every opportunity to take his case directly to the public in speeches as well as remarks made at events covered by the press. He targeted specific Senators (e.g., Mark Hatfield, OR; Ted Stevens, AL; Alfonse D'Amato, NY and Arlen Specter, PA)[267] and courted them to gain their support for the package. His senior White House staff helped to make the case as they were also quite vocal on the issue. Even the Democratic National Committee mounted a fax campaign to drum up support for the plan.

Despite the full court press put on by the administration, the economic stimulus bill was never passed. It is debatable what impact it would have had on the economy. The administration estimated that it would create 500,000 jobs[268], but analysis by some economists suggested that its impact would be minimal. A survey of chief executives who were members of the National Association of Manufacturers was very pessimistic about the President's plan[269]. On the subject of whether it would create new jobs 70% responded no. More than nine out of ten didn't think it would increase private investment and more than eight of ten didn't think it would stimulate economic growth.

However, the legislative stalemate on this issue may have set the stage for adoption of the fiscal discipline mantra that characterized the rest of the administration. Throughout the debate on the package Senate Republicans insisted that that any new spending for programs in the measure must be offset by spending cuts elsewhere. In the aftermath of economic stimulus debacle, it was pretty clear that trading cuts for new spending would be the basis of negotiations with the Republicans whose support was needed to pass the President's legislative agenda given that the Senate was so evenly divided.

The whole point of rehearsing the economic stimulus scenario is to compare President Clinton's leadership on this issue to others that had a huge impact on the nineties economic expansion. Anyone who followed the news at that time would immediately connect the Clinton administration with the economic stimulus initiative. It was central to his campaign, and upon his arrival in Washington the nation anxiously awaited a plan from the President to give a jolt to the economy. There's no question that Clinton was front and center on this issue.

By the same token, no one who kept up with the news at that time would connect the President with Y2K remediation or Telecom deregulation or the birthing of the commercial Internet. And, it is simply because he was not a prime mover on these issues. All of these things occurred on his watch, but his contribution to them was minimal at best. No one would accuse him of punishing senators for failing to support his Y2K initiatives or his Telecom reform bill. The factors that made the biggest difference economically were pretty much an afterthought for the President.

Reinventing Government

At the other end of the spectrum, there are some economically beneficial issues where the Clinton administration was definitely in the driver seat and provided high-profile leadership. A great example of this is President Clinton's initiative on reinventing government, which was chaired by Vice President Al Gore. Overall, this was a pretty successful effort and perhaps an accomplishment of the administration that doesn't get its fair share of press. The reinventing government initiative focused on enabling the federal government to run more effectively and at a reduced cost. It was launched with a comprehensive assessment of the inner workings of the federal government known as the National Performance Review (NPR), which became the nickname for the initiative. The assessment covered financial management, personnel, procurement, budgeting, and information systems among other things[270].

Upon completion of the assessment, in September 1993 the NPR commission delivered recommendations designed to shrink the civilian workforce by 252,000 employees and save $108 billion over a 5-year period[271]. Within a year of delivering these recommendations, implementation of Phase 1 of the strategy had already resulted in the reduction of 71,000 federal positions[272]. Four years later the administration claimed it had trimmed 240,000 jobs, closed approximately 2000 field offices, and achieved savings of $118 billion[273].

Of course there is some debate about the validity of these claims. For example, some of the savings claimed are forward looking, i.e., ongoing savings from structural changes projected through the year 2000. Critics also charged that a sizeable portion of the savings came from Defense. Another criticism was that more fundamental changes were needed, e.g., the elimination of entire departments, agencies or programs, and Congressional leaders offered specific recommendations about which ones. However, the progress made was enough to earn praise from some independent observers.

A year into the program, independent observers commented favorably on achievements though they also wondered whether the gains could be sustained:

> "The NPR has produced impressive results — a genuine start on changing the culture of the government. The progress is more than almost anyone, including perhaps the reinventors themselves, believed possible."[274]

The Brookings Institution

"The NPR has made remarkable progress — more than I would have expected"[275]

William Goins
Sr. VP, Xerox Corp

"The program has already gone further than previous reform efforts"[276]

Tom Shoop
Government Executive

"So far, progress has been incremental. But there are islands of improvement. The important thing is that progress is being made in bringing quality to government that hasn't occurred before."[277]

Dr. Armand Feigenbaum
Author, Total Quality Control

These accolades are significant because this was the 11th major exercise of this type since Theodore Roosevelt, and the others had not delivered results of this magnitude, including Eisenhower's Hoover Commission, Nixon's Ash Commission, and Reagan's Grace Commission.

Five years into the exercise, Donald Kettl of the Brookings Institution gave NPR an overall grade of "B" so the effort did have some staying power. Kettl gave the highest marks for improvements in the procurement process, improvements in customer service and achieving targets for downsizing the federal workforce[278]. Below is Kettl's full report card.

Performance category	Grade
Downsizing	B
Identifying objectives of government	D
Procurement reform	A
Customer service	B+
Disaster avoidance	B-
Political leadership	C+
Performance improvements	C+
Relations with Congress	D
Trust in government	C
Use of other reform models	B-
Effort	A+
Overall Grade	B

Clearly, this initiative was a priority for the President. He launched it early in his presidency (March 1993) and in a rare move appointed the Vice President to a high-profile policy role to lead the charge. Reinventing government was none other than a major exercise in quality improvement and it is well known that top-down leadership is one of the keys to success for such initiatives. That's exactly what NPR got from Clinton and Gore. The President implemented some NPR recommendations with executive orders, lobbied Congress for others and used his bully pulpit to advocate for the program. Meanwhile, the Vice President provided "hands on" leadership for the program and interfaced directly with agency heads to drive progress on targeted results. Some members of the cabinet like HUD secretary Henry Cisneros were also known as champions of the initiative[279].

Each year the White House made a lot of fanfare surrounding progress reports about the reinventing government initiative. For example, when the initial NPR report was released in September 1993, Clinton and Gore did it on the White House south lawn against a backdrop of forklifts piled high with federal rule books. In 1994 when the progress report was released the props were government issued laundry baskets overflowing with red tape[280].

And, reinventing government is a good story for the Clinton administration. It delivered solid economic results though it was not as heavy a hitter as the "Fab Five" we've outlined previously. Interestingly enough, despite the administration's efforts to showcase the initiative, the press didn't pick it up as a lead story and public awareness of NPR remained relatively low. It's also a bit puzzling why neither Clinton nor Gore made a bigger deal about this accomplishment during either the 1996 campaign or the 2000 campaign.

That said, there is still a striking difference between how NPR was handled and how the administration dealt with policy for heavy hitters like Y2K and TA-96. For example, when a telecom reform bill was first unveiled in 1994, there were no South Lawn ceremonies to promote it, no high profile point person from the executive branch to establish strategy and drive passage, no presidential courting of specific senators to influence the outcome of the bill or any of the "high-touch" strategies that were employed for top priorities of the administration.

All in all the Clinton administration's approach to items that were high on its agenda was very different than its involvement in the items that had the greatest impact on the economy of the nineties. Some of its agenda items had a positive economic impact. Others had no impact as they never made it to implementation. Still others had a net negative impact as the uncertainty surrounding them dampened economic activity even though they never made it to implementation.

Chapter 12: Lessons Learned from the '90s Economic Boom

⋰⋱

One of the reasons stated at the outset for writing this book is to provide some guidance on how some measure of the nineties prosperity can be reclaimed. Now that the critical factors that drove the boom have been revealed and the myths about Bill Clinton's role in nineties economic expansion have been dispelled, one might ask if there are any takeaways from the period that could be leveraged by policy makers going forward. You bet there are!! This chapter is devoted to discussing three key takeaway lessons:

1. New technology adoption is a powerful economic stimulus
2. Deregulation drives enormous value creation
3. Some key nineties economic catalysts won't translate to the early 21st century

New technology adoption is a powerful economic stimulus

The economic drivers of the 1980's were not as obvious as those of the 1990's, but there are some that are shared in common, confirming their effectiveness as economic catalysts. One of the economic engines of the 80's was another new technology revolution, i.e., displacement of mainframes by personal computers (PCs) as the platform for business applications and the enabler of computing for personal applications. The PC brought the power of computing to the average person's desktop. With it also came the creation of whole new industries, the birth of some of the most respected companies in existence, and greater prominence for some already well established companies, including Microsoft, Dell, Intel, Oracle, and Adobe. Several other companies that burst on the scene during that period but that have since been absorbed by other major players include Compaq and Lotus Development Corporation.

The profound economic impact of the PC revolution is indisputable. One only needs to look at the market capitalization of these companies at present. In addition to shareholder value, the PC revolution created a host of new jobs, including jobs in PC hardware, software development, peripherals R&D, industry news and analysis, and so on. For example, between 1982 and 1989 software industry jobs more than tripled growing from 112,300 to 366,400[281].

The success of the PC revolution of the '80s was repeated and "one-upped" by the Internet revolution of the '90s. In fact, the PC revolution of the '80s laid the foundation for the Internet revolution of the '90s. This raises the question of whether there is an opportunity for a trifecta i.e., a third technology revolution that can be an economic catalyst some time during the first quarter century of the new millennium.

It is safe to say that the new technology revolution in Information Technology has not yet run its course. Just like PCs paved the way for the Internet, the Internet has paved the way for a new wave of technologies to change the way world lives, works, plays, and learns to borrow a phrase from Cisco Systems. Among these are technologies waiting in the wings to break through like IP Telephony, Wireline/ Wireless integration, and mobile computing in its various forms (e.g., Smart phones, Digital media players, PDAs). Within the next decade we could see advancements in operating system architecture, data storage, speech recognition, and other computing technologies that enable the following innovations:

- Ultra-portable laptops without hard drives that boot up instantly ready for use with a flick of the "on" button like TVs. These are already on the horizon but still have some technical challenges to overcome
- Wireless phones that are as secure as wired phones, provide the same voice clarity and never drop calls
- Voice-activated handheld devices that effectively deliver functionality equivalent to desktop or laptop computers
- Home entertainment hubs that can seamlessly handle the duties of HD receiver, digital video recorder, broadband modem, computer workstation, gaming console, and digital media player as well as effortlessly connect to their single purpose counterparts and seamlessly exchange data with them
- Pen-sized storage devices capable of holding an entire computing profile (e.g., operating system, applications, user files, favorites, and preferences) and engineered to plug into smart terminals to deliver a full featured computing experience. In other words you'd be able to carry your computer desktop around in your pocket or on your wrist and enjoy the same computing experience wherever smart terminals are available, which would eventually be just about everywhere.

To the extent that one of these or another technology not mentioned here creates a fundamental change in the way the public approaches an activity like computing, communication or entertainment it has the potential to spark a whirlwind of economic activity. Take for example HDTV, sales of HD sets have been increasing at a quickening pace as we get closer to the date when broadcasters will have to transmit exclusively in digital format, but the vast majority of households have yet to purchase an HD set or other peripherals that will be required to make the transition. However, one thing is for sure those families that haven't switched over by the deadline won't suddenly stop watching TV once the conversion happens, they'll go out and purchase HD sets and the related peripherals to work with them or sign up for a digital source like cable.

Depending on which estimates one chooses to go with, as of November 2007 there were either around 31 million HD displays in US homes (per Nielsen) or around 50 million (per the Consumer Electronics Association)[282]. Meanwhile, around the same time there were over 300 million TV sets in use in the US[283]. This means somewhere in the neighborhood of 200 million sets still need to be changed out (or connected to a digital source like cable or satellite) not to mention cable set top boxes, DVD players and so on. The economic implications of this could be significant, especially if a sizeable portion of those purchases are concentrated into a short period of time.

However, the next pervasive disruptive technology may not originate in information technology. The push for US independence from foreign oil just might be the catalyst for a breakthrough in energy technology. For example, as compared with the US, Brazil has achieved phenomenal levels of ethanol usage in its transportation system. Brazil's accomplishment is the result of a focused strategy that was adopted by the government, embraced by the public, and pursued with great resolve. Along the way, automobiles in Brazil had to be outfitted with specially equipped engines and the service station infrastructure had to be built out to make dispensing of ethanol as readily available as gasoline.

If the US were to adopt a similar strategy to drive up ethanol usage, this would certainly qualify as a pervasive disruptive technology and there would be significant economic implications. Detroit would have to bring a whole new line of cars to market. In fact, this just might be the catalyst that the sluggish US automobile industry needs to get it going again. Meanwhile, there could be the emergence of a whole new aftermarket industry for retrofitting legacy engines to accommodate the new fuel. Of course as in Brazil, the service station infrastructure across the country would have to be built out. It doesn't take a rocket scientist to figure out that as Americans begin to make the transition to ethanol-enabled cars, the economic activity around this would be quite significant. It's hard to imagine a disruptive technology that will have as big an impact on society as the Internet, but this could come close. The best part of all of this is that the desire to achieve independence from foreign oil as well as to shift consumption from fossil fuels to renewable fuels has created an appetite for this type of technology shift.

But this is just the tip of the iceberg in energy technology. If the US is to achieve independence from foreign oil, it also needs breakthroughs in power generation and there are a number of exciting research and development possibilities to be pursued on this front: 1) Environmentally friendly ways of utilizing the extensive US coal supply, 2) Safe disposal of nuclear waste, which is one of the key hindrances to commissioning of nuclear power plants. None of this is going to come about by a "business as usual" approach, at least not in the short term so some creative approaches will have to be explored. Biotechnology is also fertile ground for a breakthrough in disruptive technology.

There are two key implications for public policy from the finding that new technology adoption is a powerful economic stimulus:

1) Public policy should accelerate discovery and commercialization of breakthrough technologies
2) Public policy should remove barriers to adoption of breakthrough technologies instead of erecting them

Public policy should accelerate discovery and commercialization of breakthrough technologies

Some very significant technological breakthroughs have come about as a result of publicly funded research. Earlier in the book we mentioned that MOSAIC, the forerunner of the Netscape browser, which helped to launch the Internet revolution, came about as a result of publicly funded research. MOSAIC definitely meets the bar for a significant technological breakthrough. It turns out that some other very significant technologies have also come about as a result of publicly funded research. For example, the search algorithm underlying the founding of Google has its roots in publicly funded research[284]. The same is true for the search algorithm that was the basis for the founding of Lycos[285]. Taxol, an important cancer drug, is also the product of federally funded research as is Emtriva, which is one of the components of a highly effective HIV treatment[286]. Other significant breakthroughs include MRI body scanning, the vaccine for Hepatitis B and the atomic force microscope[287].

At one point (circa 1979) patents generated as a result of federally funded research were languishing in filing cabinets as less than 5% of the available 28,000 patents had been commercialized[288]. However, in the wake of bipartisan legislation sponsored by Birch Bayh and Bob Dole, there has been a significant uptick in commercialization of patents resulting from federally funded research. According to a government report citing the General Accounting Office, during the first 20 years following passage of the bill, inventions licensed from universities and commercialized led to $30 billion of economic activity and supported 250,000 jobs[289]. This is actually a bit conservative as it does not account for the Internet effect.

Within 25 years of the passage of this legislation more than 4500 commercial companies were spun out from non-profit research institutes. In one year alone, 2004, universities reaped $1.4 billion in licensing revenues and applied for 10,000 new patents[290]. The success of this legislation encouraged other countries; including technology powerhouses like Japan and Germany to adopt similar intellectual property policies for publicly funded research as those embodied in the Bayh-Dole act[291].

To be sure Bayh-Dole is not perfect. The law has produced some controversial unintended consequences, particularly the concern that pure research is suffering as universities skew research towards projects that have the potential to produce lucrative patents. Nevertheless, Bayh-Dole does illustrate how public policy can be a catalyst for new technology invention then adoption and in turn economic growth. It also shows that to accomplish this public policy has to address four areas:

1) Enablement — There has to be funding in place to undertake research
2) Relevance / Focus — Research has to be conducted on problems that have some connection to real world applications

3) Incentives — There has to be clarity around who will benefit from research outcomes as well as a framework in place for how that policy will be operationalized
4) Successes — There have to be visible successes that give the academic research community confidence that the model works

Given what we've learned about the ability of new technology adoption to stimulate the economy as well as public policy's ability to influence invention as well as commercialization of new technologies, new technology R&D should be a pillar in the economic policy of any future administration that has the economy atop its priorities. To influence some quick wins, the incumbent administration needs a system to identify high potential research on the cusp of breaking through and approaches to get them over the hump, e.g., timed research competitions with significant awards for winners to intensify focus on these areas.

It has already been proven that an accelerated research approach can work. While it can be debated whether or not it was a good thing, the Manhattan Project produced usable nuclear weapons within six years of its launch despite numerous technical hurdles that had to be overcome. The federal government poured $2 billion ($23 billion in 2007 dollars per the Consumer Price Index) into the project, engaged 130,000 people and utilized as many as 30 research sites[292]. The same is true for a manned moon landing. This was accomplished within six years of the initiative President Kennedy kicked-off. These efforts demonstrated that concentrated focus can produce breakthroughs in a compressed time frame. Even in cases where the ultimate goal is not achieved sometimes some of the byproducts produced along the way are themselves significant advancements.

Both of these efforts were motivated by national security concerns, but given what has been learned from the nineties and eighties economies about the benefits of new technology adoption, it would make sense to apply this type of concentrated focus for economic reasons as well. What's more, since one of the promising R&D areas discussed earlier, energy technology, is considered by some to be a matter of national security, the argument for applying the accelerated research approach to this area is doubly strong.

Public policy should remove barriers to adoption of breakthrough technologies instead of erecting them

One of the reasons the impact of the Web has been so pervasive is precisely because government has resisted the urge to step in and saddle the medium with regulation that could stifle competition and creativity. For example, one reason Internet commerce has flourished is because it is largely free from taxes. Internet telephony has improved in quality and evolved into a viable alternative to other telephone options because it was allowed to develop free from the weight of regulation that constrains traditional telephone service like contributions to the universal service fund or tariffs that inflate the price of international telephone calls. Early on Internet access flourished because entrepreneurs were permitted to enter the Internet Service Providers (ISPs) business and offer service to customers without being weighed down by the complex system of regulations that govern local and long distance telephone companies even though one could argue (and some did) that ISPs provide communications services and should be subject to the same rules.

Creativity around the uses of websites mushroomed because relatively little restriction was placed on what type of information could be disseminated on the Internet or who could publish that information. Given the relatively low cost of entry and the freedom to explore, creative minds came up with a variety of uses for the Web that most people in the general public had not even imagined; a number of them in the public interest. Again one could argue that the Internet has been used for some very questionable purposes, but on balance the pros by far outweigh the cons. As a result of the government's hands-off approach to the Web, free market economics dictated the adoption and growth of the technology. The runaway success of internet adoption makes a powerful case in favor of minimizing the barriers to adoption of other breakthrough technologies.

Deregulation drives enormous value creation

We have already established the enormous value created for the American economy by telecommunications deregulation first in the eighties and then again in the nineties. Of course in the case of the second wave of telecommunications deregulation, embodied in the Telecom Act of 1996, there are some reservations about whether the legislation accomplished what it set out to do. The consensus is that it did not. Regardless, TA-96 was responsible for funneling billions of dollars into the economy as well as stimulating significant economic activity, and its foundations are still the basis on which telecommunications competition is moving forward today.

For example, cable companies, which are currently the primary competitors to incumbent local telephone companies, can compete against them precisely because of TA-96. Similarly, have you noticed that the concept of a long distance carrier has quietly disappeared? Remember the ad wars between AT&T, MCI and Sprint, each contending that it offered better prices than the others? All of that has been replaced by flat rate plans, which provide unlimited domestic long distance, again a by-product of TA-96. So despite its flaws and shortcomings, some significant value did accrue to the American public as a result of this bill.

Meanwhile, telecommunications is not the only example of an industry where deregulation has been a driver of substantial value creation. The airline industry's challenges are well known. We chide the industry about unappetizing in-flight meals, glitches with baggage handling, flight delays or cancellations and other inconveniences endured by its patrons. Yet, deregulation in that industry has also been a powerful economic catalyst.

As a result of airline deregulation, airfares have become more affordable making air travel more accessible to the general public. As might be expected, more affordable airfares have translated to increased passenger traffic, and not just more travel by the same groups of people but more travel by a broader cross-section of the public. According to one study, prior to airline deregulation half of all Americans had never flown on an airplane, but by 1988, ten years after the industry was deregulated, three quarters of Americans had[293].

Business in general has been a beneficiary of airline deregulation as affordable air travel has facilitated the conduct of business across state and international lines. Tourism and its related industries in particular have been beneficiaries as improved affordability of air travel has enabled Americans to vacation in places that were once inaccessible to them because of the high cost of airfares or the prohibitive amount of time required to get there by road. For example, prior to airline deregulation, the practice of hordes of college students descending on Florida or Caribbean beaches for Spring Break was non-existent. Now it is common practice, and despite the problems that come along with it, the Spring Break phenomenon is a boon for the travel and hospitality industries.

Open competition in the airline industry has also led to a number of innovations and enhancements that improve the quality of air travel for customers. For example, competition is responsible for carriers offering more non-stop flights as well as connections to more destinations, allowing travelers more flexibility in their schedules and shorter delays when they have to make itinerary changes due to extenuating circumstances. Open competition is also responsible for innovations like frequent traveler programs to encourage customer loyalty, as well as the practice of employing hub and spoke airports for routing passengers to cut the cost of service delivery. Airline deregulation is responsible for the birth of the discount airline, including People Express, Southwest, JetBlue, and Skybus among others. There is still quite a bit of room for improvement in airline service quality, but there is no question that competition in the industry has been a driver of service quality improvements.

The airline scenario mirrors that of telecommunications in that four major benefits for the public have resulted from deregulation of these industries: 1) Lower prices, 2) More as well as accelerated innovation, 3) Increased consumption and 4) Improved quality of life. In fact, two prominent economists, Robert Crandall and Jerry Ellig, studied five industries deregulated during the seventies, eighties and nineties (trucking, railroads, airlines, natural gas, and telecommunications) and concluded that all of them have enjoyed substantial value creation and in particular these four benefits as a result of deregulation. In the area of price relief alone, Crandall and Ellig's analysis showed that in terms of 1995 inflation adjusted dollars, Americans were saving approximately $60 billion annually as a result of the deregulation of these industries[294].

Deregulation is one of those topics that generate a lot of emotion and strong opinions on both sides of the issue. However, because so many industries have been deregulated, we have quite a bit of experience with deregulation as well as a substantial body of evidence that can be examined to determine the impact of deregulation on the economy. Pick just one of these and the merits of deregulation versus its drawbacks could be debated ad infinitum, but given the outcomes of five implementations, solid patterns and lessons have emerged that help to settle the matter. And, it is clear that the pros outweigh cons.

Part of the reason for the controversy generated by deregulation is because beyond the economic aspects of deregulation there are social aspects of deregulation as well. Among other things, regulation is in place to ensure public safety, to protect the environment, and to protect the public from unscrupulous business people as well as practices. It is important for government to stay engaged in industry to fulfill these responsibilities. However, the practice of government controlling the parameters of competition instead of letting the market decide them has been shown to be flawed.

It is also true that in the initial stages of deregulation of any industry, there is some customer pain as the business practices they're used to undergo changes. For example, when some key aspects of telecommunications were deregulated in 1984, it was a bit confusing to customers when they had to work with more than one company to get the full complement of telecommunications services they needed, particularly in business settings. Sometimes one company would come in and install phones, but after they left no one in the office could make or receive calls because the connections necessary to bring dial tone to the handsets had not been completed. Then when customers tried to find out what went wrong, providers engaged in a heavyweight bout of finger pointing, each claiming the other was responsible.

These situations were frustrating to say the least. However, most would agree the eventual payback in terms of lower prices, expanded choice of providers and new technology introduction was well worth the inconvenience they experienced at the outset of the deregulation experiment. So the notion that benefits of deregulation will be achieved without some pain is flawed, and the mere presence of customer pain does not mean that deregulation is not working. On the contrary what we have seen over and over is that when the dust settles customers are better off in the deregulated era versus the regulated one.

As of Spring 2008, there are still opportunities for economic deregulation of selected industries that could stimulate the U.S. economy including the following

- further deregulation of telecommunications
- deregulation of electrical transmission and distribution networks
- commercialization of unused or underutilized electromagnetic spectrum
- extension of airport landing rights, e.g., liberalization to include flights by international carriers

California's failed experiment with electricity reform clearly demonstrated that deregulation cannot be approached in a lackadaisical manner. However, given the similarities in the structure of the electric power industry versus telecommunications some of the benefits that have accrued to the public as a result of telecommunications deregulation could be reasonably be expected in the electric power arena as well. Policymakers should explore responsible ways to relax government control of the economic aspects of this and other promising industries to allow the magic of free market economics to work. After all, if a key aspect of protecting the public interest means enabling the public to obtain the best service for the best price, then well thought-out deregulation is part of the equation.

Some Key Nineties Economic Catalysts Won't Translate to the Early 21st Century

In the physical sciences mastery of a subject and related advancements are made possible in part by the principle that some things never change. Acids always turn litmus paper red and bases (e.g., baking soda) always turn litmus paper blue. Hydrogen and oxygen mixed together in certain specific proportions always produces water. A steel ball released from the second floor of a building will always fall toward the earth.

Not so in the world of economics. Mastery of economic policy requires a bit more creativity because economic phenomena are far less predictable. Catalysts that are effective in one context are not equally as effective in another. This is the case with some of the catalysts that played an important role in the nineties. For example, low interest rates surfaced as a powerful economic catalyst beginning 1992 and continued to have an important role in stimulating the economy all the way through the middle of the first decade of the new millennium. But, during the latter portion of the first decade and throughout the second decade of the new millennium interest rates are not likely to be as powerful of a catalyst as they were during the nineties and the early 21st century for several reasons.

Money in the Post Sub-Prime Era: Cheap? Yes, Easy to Get a Hold of? No!

First, investors are no longer looking at the real estate market through "rose colored glasses." Following the Dot-com bust, the telecom meltdown, and the subsequent stock market crash in the 2000 — 2001 time frame, historically low interest rates kept the housing market hot while other aspects of the economy were cool. In fact, after the Dot-com bust, real estate replaced the stock market as the new hot invest-ment, and in a manner of speaking the irrational exuberance that was once directed at the stock market found a new home in the realty market. Droves of new players entered the real estate market and demonstrated that there was a lot of money to be made because lots of them made out made out quite well.

However, just like with the stock market, a lot of inves-tors got burned after the Federal Reserve board raised interest rates17 consecutive times, and by 425 basis points, over a period of 24 months[295] and the housing market even-tually crashed. Now, even if interest rates are lowered again, money won't flow as readily into real estate as it once did as oodles of battered investors will be digging themselves out of the holes created by ill-advised real estate purchases. But even afterward, these folks will be painfully aware of the risks and will be much more selective about their outlays. Meanwhile, prospective new investors will be way more cautious about taking the plunge as a result of the well publi-cized setbacks experienced by others.

In other words, it is reasonable to expect that the real estate market for the most part will mirror the experience of the stock market, i.e., after the crash it will take a while to regain investors' confidence, lost ground and its upward momentum. Real estate is likely to be a bit more resilient than the stock market because of the inherent value of the investment instrument, and after all people have to have a place to live. But, there will still be a serious hangover effect from the crash that inhibits cash flow into the market.

Second, the rules of the game have changed. Even after interest rates are lowered, access to credit has tightened up. During the 14-year period from 1991 to 2005 not only did interest rates retreat to record lows, but the pool of lenders increased, the competition for borrowers' business intensi-fied, the number of loan programs multiplied and the requirements to qualify for loans were relaxed. A family could hardly have dinner without being interrupted by calls from lenders with offers to refinance their mortgages, to qualify them for home equity loans or even consolidate their student loans. Money wasn't just cheap. It was easy to get a hold of.

In the aftermath of the sub-prime crisis, all that has changed. After being forced to write off billons in defaulted loans as well as being blamed for extending credit to unqualified applicants, lenders have beefed up the requirements for obtaining a loan. In addition to this a number of lenders have gone bankrupt and many loan programs have been pulled off the market. In a nutshell, the fundamentals of borrowing and lending have changed. As a result, the influx of cash into the economy once provided by easily obtainable funds is no longer part of the equation.

Third, because interest rates stayed so low for so long and because lenders have been so aggressive at pitching refinancing deals to homeowners, there isn't nearly as large of an opportunity for refinancing as there was during the early nineties. In other words, the phenomenon that put billions of dollars back into homeowners' pockets and into the economy in the early nineties is not poised to repeat itself. Even if similar numbers of borrowers refinanced as in the early nineties, the amount of savings returned to homeowners would be much smaller because their original loan rates are much lower than the double digit rates people were trying to get out of in 1992 — 1994. As a result, Washington policymakers will have to rely on other means to put spending money back into families' pockets. Cheap money will still be an effective economic catalyst. Its effects just won't be as far reaching as they were in the nineties so it will need to be combined with other stimulus to achieve the desired effects.

One more thing on the subject of interest rates, i.e., interest rates are a double edged sword. Yes, lowering interest rates can jump start a sluggish economy. However, it is also true that rates cannot stay at rock bottom levels indefinitely for several reasons. For example, low interest rates can contribute to weakness in the dollar. So eventually interest must come up again, and it's pretty clear that the Federal Reserve board has not mastered the art of lowering and raising interest rates as a means of regulating the economy. Over the last 10 years we have been through two major cycles of interest rate hikes by the federal reserve board that were expressly designed stave off negative economic impacts. On the heels of each one, we got something as bad or worse than what was supposed to be avoided: a crash.

In the 1999-2000 time frame, the hikes were designed to give an "over heated" economy a soft landing, but instead the stock market crashed, the Dot-com bubble burst, the telecom bubble burst and the economy was sent spiraling into a recession of epic proportions. In the 2004-2006 time frame, the rate hikes were designed to control inflation and strengthen the dollar, but instead the real estate market crashed and the sub-prime crisis was set-off. In this case interest rates were more directly implicated in the badness that occurred as the higher rates produced by the hikes were partially responsible for families' inability to pay their mortgages after adjustable rates reset. Given the well established relationship between housing affordability and interest rates and given readily available information in the public record about mortgages as well as rates, this debacle should have been avoidable. With a little bit of foresight as well as application of some scholarly expertise, the regulators could have developed a model that tipped them off to the potentially severe impacts on the housing market from so many consecutive rate hikes.

Stock Options: Another One Bites the Dust

Another economic stimulant from the nineties that won't be a major player in the immediate future is stock options.

For one thing, except for a few bright spots like Google and Apple that have been rising at a meteoric pace, the lethargic upward mobility in the stock market since the crash in 2001 has left a lot of people holding options that are expiring unexercised while still under water. Also, for those options granted more recently, the lead times for them to achieve "in the money" status have slowed to the point that recipients have practically lost interest.

The fact is that without the market flying high, stock options are not as attractive a compensation tool as they once were. For example, in 2000, Cisco Systems' 401k program matched employee contributions at a rate of $1500 per year[296]. Back then who needed 401k for a retirement plan? The conventional wisdom was employees could easily retire off the appreciation from their stock options and more than a few did. By 2003 the program had changed to a more traditional match of 50¢ on the dollar up to 6% of an employee's salary[297], a subtle (and socially responsible) admission by management that stock options were no longer sufficient to satisfy employees' retirement needs.

What's more without a catalyst like the Internet revolution to drive the creation of new businesses, there aren't a lot of new start-ups entering the markets and egging on one another to hand out options to attract the best and brightest employees. However, perhaps the most significant change with respect to stock options is in the accounting rules, which requires companies to expense them. This is a real disincentive to companies to distribute options to employees on a widespread basis. As a result, options are not being handed out as broadly as they once were. In a lot of cases companies are reverting to the "old school" model when options were only reserved for top executives and some are even questioning the affordability of utilizing options for that purpose.

All of these changes in the options environment mean that the volume of options being cashed going forward won't be anywhere near their nineties levels and that the tax revenues that were generated from cashing options won't be a significant contributor to the financial health of the federal government going forward.

IT Labor Shortage: What Shortage?

Finally, the IT labor shortage that drove intense competition for resources and inspired extravagant compensation packages during the nineties will not be a factor in the near future. At the time, three powerful technology movements (Y2K Remediation, the Dot-com Revolution, and TA-96) with a voracious appetite for information technology expertise combined to create an acute shortage of IT workers. These movements waxed and waned simultaneously, and in their decline actually worked to create the reverse effect on the IT labor market. For example, with the completion of Y2K remediation, hundreds of thousands of IT workers immediately became available for other initiatives, and of course the positions that were in place for Y2K purposes were eliminated. About the same time, the Dot-com bust took thousands of positions off the table as well and also released IT staff into the job market.

Also, the short supply of IT workers during the Y2K crisis forced some companies to outsource their Y2K remediation to off-shore resources, particularly India. What came about as a result of this is reminiscent of how Japanese cars became a major factor in the U.S. automobile market. During the energy crisis in the '70s, Americans began to buy Japanese cars mainly for the fuel economy benefit. At the time, these cars were perceived to be inferior quality, but consumers soon learned that the reverse was true, that is, the Japanese cars were superior in quality to their U.S. made counterparts. As a result, sales of Japanese cars skyrocketed in the States and they have held a significant share of the U.S. automobile market ever since.

Similarly, U.S. companies utilized off-shore resources primarily for the staff augmentation benefit during the Y2K crisis and found that these programmers were more capable than they had realized as well as much less expensive. Meanwhile, massive overbuilding during the telecom boom put infrastructure at the disposal of the off-shore IT services companies for pennies on the dollar and the rise of the Internet made remote collaboration an acceptable work style. These three factors combined to help make the shortage of IT workers, which was once so prominent in the press, a distant memory and along with it the rock star status accorded to IT workers in the U.S. during the nineties. What's more is that post-2000 there isn't any compelling requirement driving an insatiable demand for IT workers. But, even if there were, an ample supply of IT expertise should be available to U.S. companies for the foreseeable future because the IT revolution continues to gain traction in country after country around the globe, and as one offshore market matures and increases in price, another less expensive and equally capable one goes online.

Epilogue

The American public remembers the nineties with fondness. It was a time of amazing prosperity and everyone would love to have that back. It's tempting to latch on to leaders who promise they can deliver that dream especially if it appears that they had something to do with creating the prosperity that was enjoyed during that period. However, the only way to reclaim the good times is to understand and apply the principles that created it. That's why this book was written. It's a buyer beware book because the conventional wisdom about the source of the Booming '90s isn't necessarily correct. You may not agree with the points of view that have been presented, but hopefully you have at least been challenged to double check the facts and determine whether you need to adjust your thinking about the source of the nineties GDP growth.

The fact of the matter is that nowadays, given the abundance of information available as well as the ease of access to it, it is customary to do due diligence on just about any purchase. Cars are thoroughly researched before they are bought, doctors are carefully researched before they are selected, medical treatments are carefully researched before they are taken, and even small household appliances are carefully researched before they are bought. Considering the magnitude of the ramifications of an economic strategy for the most prosperous nation on earth, shouldn't it be carefully researched before it is adopted? At the very least the material presented in this manuscript has sensitized you to some of the rocks you need to turn over as you evaluate alternative economic strategies.

Something else I remember with fondness are the stories I was read as child. Back then one of the things that bound us was the common stories passed down by our parents and just about every one of them had a life principle to teach. One such story was the Emperor's New Clothes. For those who might not be familiar with the story a quick recap is in order. The story is about an emperor, who was obsessed with style and high fashion. He was always decked out in the finest designer clothes and was constantly on the lookout for the next new fad. In the course of time, he was approached by a couple of swindlers posing as avant garde designers who offered to make him an outfit out of a brand new fabric that had a special quality. The fabric was invisible to anyone who was incompetent or stupid. This got the Emperor psyched. He could kill two birds with one stone, i.e., wear the finest apparel and have a way to determine which members of his cabinet were unfit for their jobs. He immediately engaged the tailors to make him an outfit out of this exotic fabric and arranged a parade for himself where he could show off his new threads to his loyal subjects.

The tailors requested all kinds of resources to carry on their work, including cash, fine food and expensive cloths. They pretended to be hard at work, but of course the new outfit was a hoax. The emperor wondered about their progress but was afraid to check on it personally because he was afraid that he might not be able to see the special fabric and we all know what that would mean. He sent some of his ministers to check the status, but for obvious reasons none of them would admit that he could not see the outfit and all reported that progress was satisfactory.

Finally, the day of the parade came and after a final flurry of activity, the tailors "completed" the outfit. There was nothing there, but since no one would admit it, the emperor included, he proceeded to remove his clothes and don the outfit that no one could see. As a result, he paraded among the crowds on the streets of his capital with no clothes on while everyone made politically correct comments about how nice his new clothes were. Only one person was daring enough to say that the emperor didn't have any clothes on, and that was a boy who was too green about social norms to know any better.

There are a lot of takeaways from this story, but the one I want to zero in on is the political correctness. Something was amiss here, but no one would say it because it wasn't the politically correct or socially acceptable thing to do. This is where the analogy breaks down a bit because in some quarters it is fashionable to bash Clintons. Nevertheless, it is hard to write about a subject like the one taken up in this book because it goes against the grain and challenges the legacy of a popular past president. Yet, on the subject of the economy, the stakes are too high to leave well enough alone. There's something wrong with the claim that Bill Clinton created 22 million jobs or that he balanced the budget. These claims have no clothes or at best are scantily dressed. Unless someone says so and brings out the facts, critical decisions about the country's future could be made on faulty grounds.

Voting is an awesome privilege enjoyed by Americans and envied by people all over the world. The American democracy thrives on the ability of the electorate to get the information they need to make informed decisions about the people and issues they vote for. As a result freedom of the press and freedom of information in general are treated as sacrosanct. Journalists are pretty much given free rein to search out and publish information that is considered to be in the public interest. Interestingly enough, the Web, one of the key topics of discussion throughout this book, has even transformed that aspect of our lives as there are now web sites (e.g., www.factcheck.org, www.politifact.com) that are devoted to investigating charges and countercharges that are made in political debates, speeches, ads as well as other campaign communications. However, even those sites do not tackle assessments of the magnitude undertaken in this work. Plus this book goes beyond just evaluation of the facts to discussion of their implications. If we would make the most of our voting privilege we should take advantage of a work like this one.

Without a doubt the topics that have been tackled have political overtones, but at its essence this is not a political book. By and large what has been attempted is to provide the public with an objective analysis that will assist their decision making process as they evaluate politicians' claims about their economic policies and what they will do for the country. The idea is to leverage lessons learned from past experiences to help people separate fact from fiction and to understand what works versus what doesn't.

In the process we have challenged the legacy of a popular past president. As a result, some might be inclined to dismiss the findings presented without giving them a fair hearing, but that would amount to a huge missed opportunity. If the conclusions drawn from our analysis are really off kilter there must be information to refute them and someone should pull it together and publish it lest the public be misled. On the other hand, if the conclusions are correct it would be an even bigger mistake to leave the conventional wisdom unchallenged. What's more, even those who disagree with the conclusions can benefit from poring over the material that has been presented because of its inherent information value.

And so this work is offered for your scrutiny. Sources have been carefully documented so that skeptics can check them. What would be most unfortunate is if the findings are dismissed without a fair hearing merely because they challenge the status quo. That result would be reminiscent of the conclusion of the Emperor's New Clothes.

Finally everyone was saying, "He doesn't have anything on!" The emperor shuddered, for he knew that they were right, but he thought, "The procession must go on!" He carried himself even more proudly, and the chamberlains walked along behind carrying the train that wasn't there.

Hans Christian Anderson
Keiserens nye klæder, 1837

Chapter 1 Notes: Myth One - The Clinton Economic Boom

1 "PRESIDENTCLINTON:ANNOUNCING20MILLION NEW JOBS CREATED AND INVESTING IN A HIGH-TECH ECONOMY." clinton3.nara.gov. December 3, 1999. http://clinton3.nara.gov/WH/Work/120399_1.html (accessed March 9, 2008).
2 Beth Nissen. "The actual 'Perfect Storm': A perfectly dreadful combination of nature's forces." www.cnn.com. June 30, 2000. http://edition.cnn.com/2000/NATURE/06/30/perfect.storm/index.html#4 (accessed July 31, 2004).

Chapter 2 Notes: The Year 2K "bug"

3 Douglas M. Bailey, Globe Staff. 1997. Profits of doom In the year 2000, a computer bug threatens to disrupt banks, airlines, and even your microwave oven. But some entrepreneurs are already making millions from it. : [City Edition]. Boston Globe. December 7, 24. http://proquest. umi.com/ (accessed July 26, 2004).

4 Jack W. Plunkett. "Plunkett's Infotech Industry Almanac 1999-2000." www.plunkettresearchonline.com. November 1998. http://www.plunkettresearchonline. com/ResearchCenter/Archives/Display.aspx?Doc=20 (accessed March 24, 2008).

5 Dewayne Lehman 2000. Senate: Y2k fixes worth the billions spent. Computerworld, March 6, 8. http://www. proquest.com/ (accessed April 22, 2008).

6 Amy Dunkin, Mary Beth Regan. 1998. A Chance That Comes Once in a Millennium. Business Week, June 29, 132. http://web3.epnet.com/ (accessed June 24, 2004).

7 Amy Dunkin, Mary Beth Regan. 1998. A Chance That Comes Once in a Millennium. Business Week, June 29, 132. http://web3.epnet.com/ (accessed June 24, 2004).

8 Steve Silberman 1998. "Y2K Bug: Older Programmers Ready, Willing, but Stable" www.wired.com. January 20. http://www.wired.com/news/print/0,1294,9767,00.html (accessed July 28, 2004).

9 Gary North 1999. "Falling Demand for Y2K Problem-Solvers - Gary North's Y2K Links and Forums." www. garynorth.com. August 28. http://www.garynorth.com/ y2k/detail_cfm/5910 (accessed July 14, 2004).

10 Thomas Hoffman, Julia King. 1999. Cobol coders miss big payday. Computerworld, January 18, 1,14. http:// proquest.umi.com/ (accessed July 27, 2004).

11 Steve Silberman 1998. "Y2K Bug: Older Programmers Ready, Willing, but Stable" www.wired.com. January 20.

http://www.wired.com/news/print/0,1294,9767,00.html (accessed July 28, 2004).

[12] Thomas Hoffman, Julia King. 1999. Cobol coders miss big payday. Computerworld, January 18, 1,14. http://proquest.umi.com/ (accessed July 27, 2004).

[13] Thomas Hoffman, Julia King. 1999. Cobol coders miss big payday. Computerworld, January 18, 1,14. http://proquest.umi.com/ (accessed July 27, 2004).

[14] Ilan Greenberg 1999. Managers turn away from retention bonuses for Y2K. InfoWorld, February 1, 74. http://proquest.umi.com/ (accessed July 30, 2004).

[15] Kirstin Downey Grimsley 1999. Y2K = Extra Pay, a Getaway; For People Who Must Work, Firms Ante Up :[FINAL Edition]. The Washington Post, December 31, http:// proquest.umi.com/ (accessed July 27, 2004).

[16] Joel Dresang 1999. Information-Technology Workers Likely to Stay in Demand after Y2K. Milwaukee Journal Sentinel, October 26. http://web3.epnet.com/ (accessed July 14, 2004).

[17] Gary North 1997. "An Extra 1,000,000 Experienced COBOL Programmers Needed - Gary North's Y2K Links and Forums." www.garynorth.com. May 21. http://www.garynorth.com/y2k/detail_cfm/135 (accessed September 8, 2004).

[18] Marianne Kolbasuk McGee 1998. Strong demand should keep salaries high. InformationWeek, August 17, 40. http://www.proquest.com/ (accessed September 7, 2004).

[19] Del Jones 2000. Y2K bug aftermath: The good, the bad, the ugly:[FINAL Edition]. USA Today, January 3, http://proquest.umi.com/ (accessed September 7, 2004).

[20] Erich Luening 1998. "Y2K war: Less time, more money." www.news.com. November 10. http://www.news.com/2102-1091_3-217723.html (accessed September 25, 2004).

21 Douglas M. Bailey, Globe Staff. 1997. Profits of doom In the year 2000, a computer bug threatens to disrupt banks, airlines, and even your microwave oven. But some entrepreneurs are already making millions from it. : [City Edition]. Boston Globe. December 7, 24. http://proquest. umi.com/ (accessed July 26, 2004).

22 StewartDeck1998.Y2Kfix-itcompanies.Computerworld, June 29, 98. http://proquest.umi.com/ (accessed July 26, 2004).

23 Douglas M. Bailey, Globe Staff. 1997. Profits of doom In the year 2000, a computer bug threatens to disrupt banks, airlines, and even your microwave oven. But some entrepreneurs are already making millions from it. : [City Edition]. Boston Globe. December 7, 24. http://proquest. umi.com/ (accessed July 26, 2004).

24 Scott Kirsner 1997. "Consultants Cash In on Computer Crash Crisis." www.wired.com. August 8. http://www. wired.com/news/print/0,1294,5686,00.html   (accessed July 28, 2004).

25 Barnaby J. Feder 1999. Companies That Danced in the Year 2000 Market Need to Find New Steps Before the Ball Ends :COUNTING TO 2000 — Betting on a Bug. New York Times, July 15, Late Edition (east Coast). http:// www.proquest.com/ (accessed September 8, 2004).

26 Scott Kirsner 1997. "Consultants Cash In on Computer Crash Crisis." www.wired.com. August 8. http://www. wired.com/news/print/0,1294,5686,00.html   (accessed July 28, 2004).

27 Bruce Caldwell, Marianne Kolbasuk McGee. 1998. Surge in services. InformationWeek, January 5, 57-62. http:// www.proquest.com/ (accessed September 8, 2004).

28 Darryl K Taft 1997. Year 2000 business builds slowly. Computer Reseller News, July 28, 10. http://www. proquest.com/ (accessed September 9, 2004).

..

[29] Laton McCartney 1998. Winning with IT consultants. Industry Week, September 7, 51-54. http://www.proquest.com/ (accessed September 9, 2004).

[30] Jennifer Waters & Steve Gelsi. "Home Depot shares sink on profit warning - MarketWatch." www.marketwatch.com. October 12, 2000. http://www.marketwatch.com/news/story/home-depot-shares-sink-profit/story.aspx?guid=%7B900FE172-2D2F-4BC0-967A-EF0953A47515%7D (accessed February 29, 2008).

[31] David Altaner 2000. Sunbeam losses mount as sales falter after Y2K rush. Sun Sentinel (Fort Lauderdale, FL), August 14. http://web3.epnet.com/ (accessed July 24, 2004).

[32] Jeff Malester 2000. Y2K sales, profit comps dog battery Big 3. TWICE, December 4, 53. http://web3.epnet.com/ (accessed July 24, 2004).

[33] Bob Howard 1999. VALLEY ROUNDUP / LAST CALL FOR Y2K; Sales of Survival Supplies Fluctuate; Retailers: Demand has increased for some gear, but in many cases business has leveled off :[Valley Edition]. Los Angeles Times, December 21, http://www.proquest.com/ (accessed July 24, 2004).

[34] Monica Toriello 1999. Y2K attack! Panic drives sales. National Home Center News, February 22, 13-14+. http://www.proquest.com/ (accessed July 24, 2004).

[35] Geof Becker 1999. Retailers get Y2K shot in arm. Marketing News, May 10, 20. http://web3.epnet.com/ (accessed July 24, 2004).

[36] Niles Steven Campbell 1998. Clinton warns of impact of Y2K computer glitch. Real Estate Finance Today, July 20, 3,22. http://www.proquest.com/ (accessed July 26, 2004).

[37] Enterprise Systems. "Countdown to Year 2000: The "Trendy Traps" of the Summer of '98." esj.com. September

1, 1998. http://esj.com/article.aspx?ID=929810604PM (accessed July 27, 2004)..

38 Douglas M. Bailey, Globe Staff. 1997. Profits of doom In the year 2000, a computer bug threatens to disrupt banks, airlines, and even your microwave oven. But some entrepreneurs are already making millions from it. : [City Edition]. Boston Globe. December 7, 24. http://proquest. umi.com/ (accessed July 26, 2004).

39 Natalie Engler 1997. Year 2000: Opportunity in adversity. Computerworld, September 15, 100-102. http://proquest. umi.com/ (accessed July 14, 2004).

40 Darryl K Taft 1997. Year 2000 business builds slowly. Computer Reseller News, July 28, 10. http://www. proquest.com/ (accessed September 9, 2004).

41 The Most Innovative IT Users. 1997. InformationWeek, September 22. http://i.cmpnet.com/infoweek/649/ graphics/introcht.pdf (accessed August 27, 2004).

42 Bob Violino 1997. IT in the Spotlight. InformationWeek, September 22. http://www.informationweek.com/649/ 500intro.htm (accessed August 27, 2004).

43 David Reichhale 1998. "Focus On Y2K Risks Up 69 Percent: Study.(by Rubin Systems) ." www.highbeam. com. July 20. http://www.highbeam.com/doc/1G1-20941146.html (accessed March 2, 2008).

44 Alison Calderbank 1997. Integrators key to year 2000 issues. Computer Reseller News, April 7, 30. http:// proquest.umi.com/ (accessed September 9, 2004).

45 Stephen Barr 1998. A Fix in Time to Keep Agencies Running; Government Plans Backup Systems, But Says Some Disruptions Are Inevitable Series: RACING THE CALENDAR: THE YEAR 2000 COMPUTER BUG Series Number: 2/3 :[FINAL Edition]. The Washington Post, August 3, http://www.proquest.com/ (accessed September 17, 2004).

[46] M.J. Zuckerman 1998. Government earns an 'F' for fixing Year 2000 woes; [FINAL edition]. USA Today, June 3. http://proquest.umi.com/ (accessed July 26, 2004).

[47] Frank Wolfe 1997. PENTAGON NOT ON TRACK TO FIX Y2K PROBLEM UNTIL 2012, HORN SAYS. Defense Daily, December 12, 1. http:// proquest.umi. com/ (accessed September 17, 2004).

[48] Darryl K Taft 1997. Year 2000 business builds slowly. Computer Reseller News, July 28, 10. http://www. proquest.com/ (accessed September 9, 2004).

[49] Alison Calderbank 1997. Integrators key to year 2000 issues. Computer Reseller News, April 7, 30. http:// proquest.umi.com/ (accessed September 9, 2004).

[50] Stephen Barr 1998. A Fix in Time to Keep Agencies Running; Government Plans Backup Systems, But Says Some Disruptions Are Inevitable Series: RACING THE CALENDAR: THE YEAR 2000 COMPUTER BUG Series Number: 2/3 :[FINAL Edition]. The Washington Post, August 3, http://proquest.umi.com/ (accessed September 17, 2004).

Chapter 3 Notes: Creation of the World Wide Web and a User Friendly Interface to Access It: The Browser

[51] Bill Clinton. President's Speech 10/02/96. October 10, 1996. http://govinfo.library.unt.edu/npr/library/speeches/101096.html (accessed March 6, 2008).

[52] Robert D. Hof. "The eBay Economy." www.businessweek.com. August 25, 2003. http://www.businessweek.com/print/magazine/content/03_34/b3846650.htm (accessed July 5, 2004).

[53] Online shopping up 19%. 2008. Furniture Today, January 21, 66. http://www.proquest.com/ (accessed April 17, 2008).

[54] Vint Cerf. "Internet Society (ISOC) All About The Internet: History of the Internet." www.isoc.org. February 5, 2008. http://www.isoc.org/internet/history/cerf.shtml (accessed April 7, 2008).

[55] Internet World Stats. "Internet Growth Statistics - Global Village Online." www.internetworldstats.com. October 18, 2007. http://www.internetworldstats.com/emarketing.htm#stats (accessed 18 October, 2007).

[56] Internet World Stats. "Internet Growth Statistics - Global Village Online." www.internetworldstats.com. October 18, 2007. http://www.internetworldstats.com/emarketing.htm#stats (accessed 18 October, 2007).

[57] Cisco Systems and University of Texas. "Measuring the Internet Economy." momentumresearchgroup.com. January 2001. http://momentumresearchgroup.com/downloads/reports/internet-indicators-2001.pdf (accessed November 20, 2007).

[58] Cisco Systems and University of Texas. "Measuring the Internet Economy." momentumresearchgroup.com. January 2001. http://momentumresearchgroup.com/downloads/reports/internet-indicators-2001.pdf (accessed November 20, 2007).

59 Cisco Systems and University of Texas. "Measuring the Internet Economy." momentumresearchgroup. com. January 2001. http://momentumresearchgroup. com/downloads/reports/internet-indicators-2001.pdf (accessed November 20, 2007).
60 Cisco Systems and University of Texas. "Measuring the Internet Economy." momentumresearchgroup. com. January 2001. http://momentumresearchgroup. com/downloads/reports/internet-indicators-2001.pdf (accessed November 20, 2007).
61 Cisco Systems and University of Texas. "Measuring the Internet Economy." momentumresearchgroup. com. January 2001. http://momentumresearchgroup. com/downloads/reports/internet-indicators-2001.pdf (accessed November 20, 2007).
62 Elizabeth Gardner. "Pay Day! The Compensation Climate." Internet World, July 1, 2001: 26-33.
63 Eve Epstein and Sandy Kolste. 2000. Dot-coms revamp salary landscape. InfoWorld, June 26, 108-112. http:// www.proquest.com/ (accessed August 5, 2004).
64 Diane E. Lewis 2000. Dot-Coms, Old-Line Firms Battle for Best and Brightest at Stake, Lure of Quick Riches vs. Stability. The Boston Globe, April 16, http://proquest. umi.com/ (accessed August 5, 2004).
66 Denise Gellene 2000. COLUMN ONE; Geekdom Is Awash in Perks; With stock options no longer doing the trick, desperate 'dot-coms' are luring programmers with big salaries, free trips and on-the-job luxuries :[Home Edition]. Los Angeles Times, May 23, http://www. proquest.com/ (accessed August 5, 2004).
67 Bob Violino and Jennifer Mateyaschuk. "Labor Intensive: An increasing IT labor shortage calls for creative ways to do more with less." www.informationweek.com. July 5, 1999. http://www.informationweek.com/742/labor.htm (accessed July 14, 2004).

67 Denise Gellene 2000. COLUMN ONE; Geekdom Is Awash in Perks; With stock options no longer doing the trick, desperate 'dot-coms' are luring programmers with big salaries, free trips and on-the-job luxuries :[Home Edition]. Los Angeles Times, May 23, http://www.proquest.com/ (accessed August 5, 2004).

68 David Leonhardt 2000. Law Firms' Pay Soars to Stem Dot-Com Defections. New York Times, February 2, Late Edition (east Coast). http://www.proquest.com/ (accessed August 5, 2004).

69 David Leonhardt 2000. And Let the Lawyers Sing: 'Glory to the Salary King'. New York Times, February 4, Late Edition (east Coast). http://www.proquest.com/ (accessed August 5, 2004).

70 Phat X. Chiem 2000. The Dot-com Brain Drain Employees of the Best Known Consulting Firms are Leaving for Internet Start-ups, Forcing the Button-Down Advisers to Re-Evaluate Incentives. Chicago Tribune, May 9, Chicago Sports Final, N Edition. http:// proquest.umi.com/ (accessed August 5, 2004).

71 Phat X. Chiem 2000. The Dot-com Brain Drain Employees of the Best Known Consulting Firms are Leaving for Internet Start-ups, Forcing the Button-Down Advisers to Re-Evaluate Incentives. Chicago Tribune, May 9, Chicago Sports Final, N Edition. http:// proquest.umi.com/ (accessed August 5, 2004).

72 Laura Petrecca and Alice Z Cuneo. 1999. Bigger salaries, important titles lure away talent. Advertising Age, December 6, S6-S8. http://www.proquest.com/ (accessed August 5, 2004).

73 OLAF de SENERPONT DOMIS 1999. Survey Finds 60% Of Bank Managers Hunting New Jobs. American Banker, December 29, http://www.proquest.com/ (accessed August 5, 2004).

[74] Jennifer Weitzman 2000. Dot-Com Defectors: Not Just Money Moved Them. American Banker, March 30, http://www.proquest.com/ (accessed March 4, 2008).

[75] Technology Boom Brings Explosion of Low-Wage Jobs to California. 2000. The Record, April 19, 28. http://web3.epnet.com/ (accessed August 5, 2004).

[76] Foreign Investment Spurs Region's Employment Prospects :[All 03/24/93 Edition]. 1993. Christian Science Monitor (pre-1997 Fulltext), March 24, http://www.proquest.com/ (accessed December 8, 2007).

[77] Technology 21. "Technology 21 The Keystone Spirit: Putting Technology To Work." sites.state.pa.us. January 21, 1998. http://sites.state.pa.us/PA_Exec/DCED/tech21/tech21m.pdf (accessed December 4, 2007).

[78] Michael J. Mandel, With Andy Reinhardt in San Francisco and bureau reports. 1997. The New Business Cycle :It used to be housing and autos. But now, high tech rules. And a stall there could stagger the economy. Business Week, March 31, 58. http://www.proquest.com/ (accessed March 4, 2008).

[79] Stephen B. Pociask. "Building a Nationwide Broadband Network: Speeding Job Growth." www.newmillennium-research.org. February 25, 2002. http://www.newmillenniumresearch.org/event-02-25-2002/jobspaper.pdf (accessed November 27, 2007).

[80] Bob Hagen. "Netscape Buying Frenzy Reflects New Investment Model." Inside Tucson Business, August 21, 1995: 9.

[81] Andrew E. Serwer 1995. FURTHER FALLOUT FROM LAST WEEK'S NUTTY NETSCAPE IPO. Fortune, September 4. http://money.cnn.com/magazines/fortune/fortune_archive/1995/09/04/205894/index.htm (accessed March 6, 2008).

82 Hale and Dorr, LLP. 2001 IPO Report. July 15, 2002. http://www.altassets.com/pdfs/2001_IPO_HaleDorr.pdf (accessed October 12, 2007).

83 Matt Krantz 1999. IPO highfliers continue gains First-day doublers part of craze, analysts say, [FINAL Edition]. USA Today, December 8, http://proquest.umi.com/ (accessed September 6, 2004).

84 Michael Liedtke 2001. First-quarter venture capital investments fall to two-year low. Associated Press, May 2. http://www.sfgate.com/cgi-bin/article.cgi?file=/news/archive/2001/05/02/financial1514edt0215.dtl (accessed July7, 2004).

85 New York Times. "200 Venture Funds Were Started This Year ." http://query.nytimes.com. December 28, 2001. http://query.nytimes.com/gst/fullpage.html?res=9907E5DC1131F93BA15751C1A9679C8B63 (accessed March 8, 2008).

86 Barbara Rose 2001. Venture Capital Group Finds Investments Led to Millions of Jobs Since 1970. Chicago Tribune, October 22. http:// proquest.umi.com/ (accessed July 13, 2004).

87 John Wyatt 1996. America's amazing IPO bonanza. Fortune, May 27, 76. http:// proquest.umi.com/ (accessed September 6, 2004).

Chapter 4 Notes: The Telecom Act of 1996

[88] 4tele.net. "Telecommunications Act of 1996." *www.best-4u.com*. http://best-4u.com/4tele/act1996.htm (accessed November 23, 2007).

[89] Steve Lohr 1992. William McGowan Is Dead at 64; A Challenger of Phone Monopoly :[Biography; Obituary (Obit)]. New York Times, June 9, Late Edition (east Coast). http://www.proquest.com/ (accessed February 19, 2008).

[90] The Biggest and the Best Users of IT. 1995. InformationWeek, September 18. http://i.cmpnet.com/ infoweek/545/graphics/iw500u.pdf (accessed October 27, 2007).

[91] James Zolnierek, Katie Rangos, and James Eisner. Long Distance Market Shares Fourth Quarter 1998. FCC Common Carrier Bureau Industry Analysis, Washington, D.C.: Federal Communications Commission, 1999.

[92] The Biggest and the Best Users of IT. 1995. InformationWeek, September 18. http://i.cmpnet.com/ infoweek/545/graphics/iw500u.pdf (accessed October 27, 2007).

[93] Shira McCarthy 1995. Long-distance war of words heats up. Telephony, May 22, 14. http://www.proquest.com/ (accessed November 20, 2007).

[94] Trends in telephone service. 1996. Federal Communications Commission, May, Table 28 http:// www.cs.columbia.edu/~hgs/internet/trend196/trend196. html (accessed November 20, 2007).

[95] Robert Crandall and Jerry Ellig 1997. Economic Deregulation and Customer Choice: Lessons for the Electric Industry. Mercatus Center at George Mason University. January 1. http://www.mercatus.org/repository/docLib/MC_RSP_RP-Dregulation_970101.pdf (accessed October 27, 2007).

96 Robert Crandall and Jerry Ellig 1997. Economic Deregulation and Customer Choice: Lessons for the Electric Industry. Mercatus Center at George Mason University. January 1. http://www.mercatus.org/repository/docLib/MC_RSP_RP-Dregulation_970101.pdf (accessed October 27, 2007).

97 Trendsintelephoneservice.1996.FederalCommunications Commission, May, http://www.cs.columbia.edu/~hgs/internet/trend196/trend196.html (accessed November 20, 2007).

98 Paul F. Kirvan 1994. Divestiture: Its impact on end users. Communications News, January 1, 11. http://www.proquest.com/ (accessed November 20, 2007).

99 Rebecca Blumenstein 2000. How the Split-Up Touched Everyone —- AT&T's Splintering Spurred Rate Drop and Innovation But Hurt Customer Service. Wall Street Journal, June 6, Eastern Edition. http://www.proquest.com/ (accessed November 20, 2007).

100 William E.Kennard 2000. "Telecommunications @ the Millennium: The Telecom Act At Four; Hot Links To An Open Society". February 8. http://www.fcc.gov/Speeches/Kennard/2000/spwek005.html (accessed June 2, 2007).

101 Trends in telephone service. 1996. Federal Communications Commission, May, Table 21 http://www.cs.columbia.edu/~hgs/internet/trend196/trend196.html (accessed November 20, 2007).

102 Peter J. Howe Globe Staff. 1999. "Breakup, then buildup As with any revolution, things got messy but many consider Bell move a ringing success." Boston Globe. June 6, F1. http://proquest.umi.com (accessed June 15, 2004).

103 New York Stock Exchange. Daily Stock Price Record - 1983 - October November December. New York: Standard and Poor's Corporation, 1983.

[104] US History Encyclopedia. "AT&T Corporation: Information and Much More from Answers.com." Answers.com. 21 2008, February. http://www.answers.com/topic/at-t-corporation?cat=biz-fin (accessed 21 2008, February).

[105] Pablo Galarza 1996. Happy Independence Day. Financial World, April 22, 38. http://www.proquest.com/ (accessed October 23, 2007).

[106] Toll-Free, Pre-Paid Markets Boom; 900 On The Rebound. 1998. Advanced Intelligent Network News, March 18, 1. http://www.proquest.com/ (accessed October 23, 2007).

[107] Rebecca Conklin 1995. Listening for Ring of Success. Boston Globe, January 11, http://www.proquest.umi.com/ (accessed August 14, 2004).

[108] ISP-Planet. "Competitors Made Gains, Still Face Challenges, ALTS Report Says." *ISP-Planet.com*. February 3, 2000. http://isp-planet.com/cplanet/news/0002/000203alts.htm (accessed August 15, 2004).

[109] ISP-Planet. "Competitors Made Gains, Still Face Challenges, ALTS Report Says." *ISP-Planet.com*. February 3, 2000. http://isp-planet.com/cplanet/news/0002/000203alts.htm (accessed August 15, 2004).

[110] New Paradigm Resources Group. "Measuring the Economic Impact of the Telecommunications Act of 1996: Telecommunication Capital Expenditures (1996-2001)." *www.comptel.org*. October 2002. http://www.comptelascent.org/public-policy/position-papers/documents/capex_report_oct_2002.pdf (accessed November 23, 2007).

[111] New Paradigm Resources Group. "Measuring the Economic Impact of the Telecommunications Act of 1996: Telecommunication Capital Expenditures (1996-2001)." www.comptel.org. October 2002. http://www.comptelascent.org/public-policy/position-papers/docu-

ments/capex_report_oct_2002.pdf (accessed November 23, 2007).

[112] Ted McKenna 2001. Piecing together the OSS. Telecommunications Americas, September 1, 36-40. http://www.proquest.com/ (accessed February 21, 2008).

[113] Christopher Carbone 2006. Cutting the Cord: Telecommunications Employment Shifts Toward Wireless. Monthly Labor Review, July. http://www.bls. gov/opub/mlr/2006/07/art3full.pdf (accessed November 24, 2007).

[114] Christopher Carbone 2006. Cutting the Cord: Telecommunications Employment Shifts Toward Wireless. Monthly Labor Review, July. http://www.bls. gov/opub/mlr/2006/07/art3full.pdf (accessed November 24, 2007).

[115] Progress Report: Growth and Competition in U.S. Telecommunications. 1999. Council of Economic Advisors, February 8. http://www.ntia.doc.gov/ntia-home/press/ceafinalrpt.htm (accessed June 2, 2007).

[116] 4tele.net. "Telecommunications Act of 1996." *www.best-4u.com*. http://best-4u.com/4tele/act1996.htm (accessed November 23, 2007).

[117] Edmund L. Andrews 1995. Kerrey Vows to Stall Telecommunications Bill. New York Times, June 9, Late Edition (east Coast). http://www.proquest.com/ (accessed August 14, 2004).

[118] Jube Shiver Jr. 1994. Telecommunications Bill Faces Extinction in Senate Congress: Measure languishes due to bitter debate between Baby Bells and Sen. Ernest Hollings :[Home Edition]. Los Angeles Times (pre-1997 Fulltext), August 5, http://www.proquest.com/ (accessed August 17, 2004).

[119] Progress Report: Growth and Competition in U.S. Telecommunications. 1999. Council of Economic

Advisors, February 8. http://www.ntia.doc.gov/ntiahome/ press/ceafinalrpt.htm (accessed June 2, 2007).

[120] Richard Evans 1996. Free at last. Barron's, July 8, 18. http://www.proquest.com/ (accessed August 14, 2004).

[121] Organisation for Economic Co-operation and Development. OECD Communications Outlook 2001. Paris: Organisation for Economic Co-operation and Development, 2001.

[122] Organisation for Economic Co-operation and Development. OECD Communications Outlook 2001. Paris: Organisation for Economic Co-operation and Development, 2001.

[123] Organisation for Economic Co-operation and Development. OECD Communications Outlook 2001. Paris: Organisation for Economic Co-operation and Development, 2001.

[124] Organisation for Economic Co-operation and Development. OECD Communications Outlook 2003. Paris: Organisation for Economic Co-operation and Development, 2003.

[125] Kathy Brister 2002. "State's telecom initiative on idle." Atlanta Journal and Constitution. August 16, C1. http:// www.proquest.umi.com/ (accessed September 7, 2004).

Chapter 5 Notes: Cheap Money

[126] Lucinda Harper and Erle Norton 1993. Economic R3 Business, April 1, 1-11. http://www.proquest.com/ (accessed March 30, 2008).

[134] Jennifer L. Martel and David S. Langdon. "The Job Market in 2000: slowing down as the year ended." Monthly Labor Review, February 2001: 3-30.

[135] Edwin Meese III . "The Leadership of Ronald Reagan." www.thereaganlegacy.com. March 25, 1999. http://www.thereaganlegacy.com/version2/commentarydetails.asp?sID=8&artID=1 (accessed July 4, 2007).

[136] Mitchell Pacelle 1992. Refinancing Of Mortgages Shows a Decline —- Volume Has Skidded 50% Since September as Rates Have Increased 1/2 Point. Wall Street Journal, November 23, Eastern Edition. http://www.proquest.com/ (accessed June 30, 2007).

[137] Jim Carlton 1992. Mortgage Refinancing Boom Is Expected to Continue Whoever Wins the Election. Wall Street Journal, October 19, Eastern Edition. http://www.proquest.com/ (accessed June 30, 2007).

[138] Ted Cornwell 1995. Refis helped cut deficit. National Mortgage News, May 1, 1. http://www.proquest.com/ (accessed June 30, 2007).

[139] William F. Powers 1992. Rates Spark New Rush to Refinance; Cheaper Mortgages Also Draw Some Cautious Home Buying :[FINAL Edition]. The Washington Post (pre-1997 Fulltext), July 24, http://www.proquest.com/ (accessed June 30, 2007).

[140] Marianne Kyriakos 1994. Mortgage Refinancing Set Record Pace in 1993; Heading Into the New Year, Lenders Face a Drop in Volume as Boom Wanes :[FINAL Edition]. The Washington Post (pre-1997 Fulltext), January 8, http://www.proquest.com/ (accessed June 30, 2004).

[141] James L. Tyson, Staff writer of The Christian Science Monitor 1998. Falling Interest Rates Pour Cash Into Economy :[ALL 01/12/98 Edition]. Christian Science Monitor, January 12, http://www.proquest.com/ (accessed July 8, 2007).

[142] Edward Kulkosky 1995. Lingering Effects of the Refi Boom Seen Blunting Impact of Fed Hikes. American Banker (pre-1997 Fulltext), March 15, http://www. proquest.com/ (accessed June 30, 2007).

[143] Ted Cornwell 1995. Refis helped cut deficit. National Mortgage News, May 1, 1. http://www.proquest.com/ (accessed June 30, 2007).

[144] Marianne Kyriakos 1994. Mortgage Refinancing Set Record Pace in 1993; Heading Into the New Year, Lenders Face a Drop in Volume as Boom Wanes :[FINAL Edition]. The Washington Post (pre-1997 Fulltext), January 8, http://www.proquest.com/ (accessed June 30, 2007).

[145] Ellen Stark 1998. Cut your mortgage down to size. Money, March 1, 96-103. http://find.galegroup.com/ (accessed July 21, 2007).

[146] Jim Carlton 1992. Mortgage Refinancing Boom Is Expected to Continue Whoever Wins the Election. Wall Street Journal, October 19, Eastern Edition. http://www. proquest.com/ (accessed June 30, 2007).

[147] David Berson. "State of the Economy: Regional and National - MBA National Servicing Conference." www. mortgagebankers.org. February 15, 2006. http://www. mortgagebankers.org/files/Conferences/2006/Servicing/ StateoftheEconomy_DavidBerson.ppt#344,20,MBA (accessed October 9, 2007).

[148] Servicers show concern about refi and secondary market issues. 1999. National Mortgage News, March 8, 28. http://www.proquest.com/ (accessed February 5, 2008).

[149] Joseph Rebello 2000. Financing Boom Didn't Set Off A Spending Binge. Wall Street Journal, July 18, Eastern

Edition. http://www.proquest.com/ (accessed February 5, 2008).

150 Mitchell Pacelle 1992. Homeowners Are Rushing To Refinance —- But Fed's Interest-Rate Cut Hasn't Spurred Frenzy In Loans to Buy Houses. Wall Street Journal, July 21, Eastern Edition. http://www.proquest.com/ (accessed June 30, 2007).

151 Mitchell Pacelle 1992. Refinancing Of Mortgages Shows a Decline —- Volume Has Skidded 50% Since September as Rates Have Increased 1/2 Point. Wall Street Journal, November 23, Eastern Edition. http://www.proquest.com/ (accessed June 30, 2007).

152 Will the Mortgage Refinancing Binge Ever Stop? 1992. Banking Management, September 1, 22. http://www.proquest.com/ (accessed June 30, 2007).

153 Mitchell Pacelle 1992. Refinancing Of Mortgages Shows a Decline —- Volume Has Skidded 50% Since September as Rates Have Increased 1/2 Point. Wall Street Journal, November 23, Eastern Edition. http://www.proquest.com/ (accessed June 30, 2007).

154 Jim Carlton 1993. Late payments on home mortgages tumbled during the fourth quarter. Wall Street Journal, March 4, Eastern Edition. http://www.proquest.com/ (accessed June 30, 2007).

155 Albert R. Karr 1993. Home Building Ended the Year With a Bounce —- Reduced Mortgage Rates, Improved Psychology Helped Housing Starts. Wall Street Journal, January 25, Eastern Edition. http://www.proquest.com/ (accessed July 27, 2007).

156 U.S. Department of Housing and Urban Development. U.S. Housing Market Conditions, Fourth Quarter 2001: Historical Data, Table 7. October 20, 2007. http://www.huduser.org/periodicals/ushmc/winter2001/histdat07.htm (accessed October 20, 2007).

157 Home improvement booms in 1993. 1994. Chain Store Age Executive with Shopping Center Age 2, August 1, 14A. http://www.proquest.com/ (accessed September 30, 2007).

158 Ray Wise 1994. Playing the housing recovery obliquely. Pension World, January 1, 8. http://www.proquest.com/ (accessed September 30, 2007).

159 Lucinda Harper and Erle Norton 1993. Economic Recovery Picking Up Steam —- Jobless Rate Skids to 6.4% As Firms Add Workers; Interest Rates Are Key. Wall Street Journal, December 6, Eastern Edition.

160 Ray Wise 1994. Playing the housing recovery obliquely. Pension World, January 1, 8. http://www.proquest.com/ (accessed September 30, 2007).

161 Joseph Spiers 1994. How the Fed's latest rate hike will dent the economy. Fortune, September 19, 27. http://www.proquest.com/ (accessed September 3, 2007).

162 U.S. Department of Housing and Urban Development. U.S. Housing Market Conditions, Fourth Quarter 2001: Historical Data, Table 7. October 20, 2007. http://www.huduser.org/periodicals/ushmc/winter2001/histdat07.htm (accessed October 20, 2007).

163 The Associated Press 1993. HOUSING STARTS JUMP AS INTEREST RATES STAY LOW :[FINAL Edition]. Seattle Post - Intelligencer, September 22, http://www.proquest.com/ (accessed September 10, 2007).

164 Lucinda Harper and Erle Norton 1993. Economic Recovery Picking Up Steam —- Jobless Rate Skids to 6.4% As Firms Add Workers; Interest Rates Are Key. Wall Street Journal, December 6, Eastern Edition. http://www.proquest.com/ (accessed September 3, 2007).

165 Low Mortgage Rates Push Up Housing Starts. 1993. New York Times, October 20, Late Edition (east Coast). http://www.proquest.com/ (accessed July 27, 2007).

[166] The Associated Press 1993. SALES OF EXISTING HOMES UP 8.7 PCT. DECEMBER FLURRY PUT RATE AT 13-YEAR HIGH :[FINAL Edition]. Seattle Post - Intelligencer, January 27, http://www.proquest.com/ (accessed August 21, 2007).

[167] Joseph Spiers 1992. A Boom in '93? Yes, for Business Spending. No, for the Economy. Fortune, December 14, 25. http://www.proquest.com/ (accessed September 3, 2007).

[168] Rob Norton 1993. The U.S. economy begins to crawl from the mire. Fortune, November 1, 21. http://www.proquest.com/ (accessed September 3, 2007).

[169] Howard Banks 1993. What's ahead for business. Forbes, September 27, 37. http://www.proquest.com/ (accessed September 3, 2007).

[170] Kevin Kelly 1994. Hand-over-fist capital spending. Business Week: Industrial/Technology, February 14, 28. http://global.factiva.com/ha/default.aspx (accessed September 3, 2007).

[171] John M. Berry 1995. A Spending Boom Equips the Economy for Future Growth :[FINAL Edition]. The Washington Post (pre-1997 Fulltext), May 4, http://www.proquest.com/ (accessed September 3, 2007).

[172] Kevin Kelly 1994. Hand-over-fist capital spending. Business Week: Industrial/Technology, February 14, 28. http://global.factiva.com/ha/default.aspx (accessed September 3, 2007).

[173] Board of Governors of the Federal Reserve System. "Federal Reserve Statistical Release - Selected Interest Rates (Monthly)." www.federalreserve.gov. July 2007, 23. http://www.federalreserve.gov/releases/h15/data/Monthly/H15_FF_O.txt (accessed July 29, 2007).

[174] High anxiety. Sept 6, 1993 v45 n17 p14(1)National Review, 45, n17. p.14(1). http://find.galegroup.com/ (accessed July 30, 2007).

175 Jim Carlton 1992. Mortgage Refinancing Boom Is Expected to Continue Whoever Wins the Election. Wall Street Journal, October 19, Eastern Edition. http://www.proquest.com/ (accessed June 30, 2007).

176 Affordability Index Rises. 1993. New York Times, February 13, Late Edition (east Coast). http://www.proquest.com/ (accessed August 14, 2007).

177 Mark M Zandi, Celia Chen, Wesley Basel. 1998. A balanced yet booming market. Mortgage Banking, September 1, 22-38. http://www.proquest.com/ (accessed February 6, 2008).

178 Hobart Rowen 1993. Clinton Softens Rate Cut Claim :[FINAL Edition]. The Washington Post (pre-1997 Fulltext), August 15, http://www.proquest.com/ (accessed July 29, 2007).

179 Owen Ullmann 1993. CLINTON CAN `PARTY' OVER DROP IN RATES :[FINAL Edition]. Seattle Times, February 24, http://www.proquest.com/ (accessed July 30, 2007).

Chapter 6 Notes: Large pool of unsophisticated investors

[180] David Friedman 1998. The Newest S&L; Rather than save the old-fashioned way, more Americans depend on Wall Street to finance their retirements. Can government allow a bear market :[Home Edition]. Los Angeles Times, November 22, http://www.proquest.com/ (accessed August 21, 2004).

[181] Trevor Thomas 2000. ICI study finds surge in fund ownership. National Underwriter, September 18, 8,16. http://www.proquest.com/ (accessed October 30, 2007).

[182] Thomas S. Mulligan 1998. Theory of Cycles Helps Put Stock Slump in Context; Economics: The wave that recently hit markets is similar to those of real-estate and other past fluctuations :[Home Edition]. Los Angeles Times, September 6, http://www.proquest.com/ (accessed August 20, 2004).

[183] Ownership of Mutual Funds at New Peak. 2000. New York Times, September 6, Late Edition (east Coast). http://www.proquest.com/ (accessed August 5, 2004).

[184] NYSE. "Shareownership 2000." www.nyse.com. December 8, 2000. http://www.nyse.com/pdfs/shareho.pdf (accessed April 16, 2008).

[185] Ron Chernow 1998. Hard-Charging Bulls and Red Flags :[Op-Ed]. New York Times, September 2, Late Edition (east Coast). http://www.proquest.com/ (accessed August 22, 2004).

[186] Kathy M. Kristof 1999. YOUR MONEY; INVESTING 201; Some See Information Highway as Road to Riches, Others as Road to Ruin Series: This is the third lesson in Investing 201, a 10-part series that looks at changes in the investing landscape that have occurred over the last few years. Lesson 3 focuses on Internet stocks. Next week: Online investing :[Home Edition]. Los Angeles

Times, May 16, http://www.proquest.com/ (accessed August 21, 2004).

[187] Joel Palmer 2000. Whom Should You Bet On? Des Moines Business Record, November 06, 13-18. http://web14.epnet.com/ (accessed August 22, 2004).

[188] Kathy M. Kristof 1999. YOUR MONEY; INVESTING 201; Some See Information Highway as Road to Riches, Others as Road to Ruin Series: This is the third lesson in Investing 201, a 10-part series that looks at changes in the investing landscape that have occurred over the last few years. Lesson 3 focuses on Internet stocks. Next week: Online investing :[Home Edition]. Los Angeles Times, May 16, http://www.proquest.com/ (accessed August 21, 2004).

[189] Thomas S. Mulligan 1998. Theory of Cycles Helps Put Stock Slump in Context; Economics: The wave that recently hit markets is similar to those of real-estate and other past fluctuations :[Home Edition]. Los Angeles Times, September 6, http://www.proquest.com/ (accessed August 20, 2004).

[190] Thomas S. Mulligan 1998. Theory of Cycles Helps Put Stock Slump in Context; Economics: The wave that recently hit markets is similar to those of real-estate and other past fluctuations :[Home Edition]. Los Angeles Times, September 6, http://www.proquest.com/ (accessed August 20, 2004).

[191] Shawn Tully and Ani Hadjian 1996. HOW TO MAKE $400,000,000 IN JUST ONE MINUTE... ...AND OTHER TALES FROM THE RAREFIED WORLD OF VENTURE CAPITALISTS. THESE BEHIND-THE-SCENES, RISK-LOVING WIZARDS ARE DRIVING THE IPO CRAZE WITH HIGH-TECH STARTUPS LIKE NETSCAPE AND YAHOO. Fortune, May 27. http://money.cnn.com/magazines/fortune/fortune_arch

ive/1996/05/27/212866/index.htm (accessed March 16, 2008).

192 Adam Bryant 1999. They're rich (and you're not). Newsweek, July 5, 36-43. http://proquest.umi.com/ (accessed August 20, 2004).

193 Adam Bryant 1999. They're rich (and you're not). Newsweek, July 5, 36-43. http://proquest.umi.com/ (accessed August 20, 2004).

194 John Sleeman, Jim Rodgers, Blair Feltman, Jonny Cheecham. 2001. Do you own stocks? Saturday Night, February 3, 15. http://www.proquest.com/ (accessed August 21, 2004).

195 Jane Bryant Quinn 1999. Dumb luck on Wall Street. Newsweek, July 5, 45. http://www.proquest.com/ (accessed August 22, 2004).

196 Greg Ip 1998. It's Official: Stock Market's Pups Are Likely to Be Bulls. Wall Street Journal, July 8, Eastern Edition. http://www.proquest.com/ (accessed February 12, 2008).

197 John Leland 1998. Blessed by the bull. Newsweek, April 27, 50-53. http://web14.epnet.com/ (accessed August 20, 2004).

198 John Leland 1998. Blessed by the bull. Newsweek, April 27, 50-53. http://web14.epnet.com/ (accessed August 20, 2004).

199 Lexington: Al Gore's investor problem. 2000. The Economist, October 21, 41. http://www.proquest.com/ (accessed August 14, 2004).

200 Ron Chernow 1998. Hard-Charging Bulls and Red Flags :[Op-Ed]. New York Times, September 2, Late Edition (east Coast). http://www.proquest.com/ (accessed August 22, 2004).

201 Kimberly Blanton, Globe Staff 2000. "AMERICANS' ARDOR FOR STOCK UNSHAKEN BY MARKET VOLATILITY INVESTORS PUT RECORD $54

BILLION IN EQUITY MUTUAL FUNDS IN FEBRUARY."
[202] John Leland 1998. Blessed by the bull. Newsweek, April 27, 50-53. http://web14.epnet.com/ (accessed August 20, 2004).
[203] Barbara Sullivan 1997. New Investors Stay Cool in Wake of Stocks' Slide 'We're in for Long Haul,' They Say; [Chicagoland Final Edition]. Chicago Tribune, April 6. http:// proquest.umi.com/ (accessed August 21, 2004).
[204] Gretchen Morgenson 1999. Day Trades: Big Growth, Big Risks. New York Times, July 31, Late Edition (east Coast). http://proquest.umi.com/ (accessed August 21, 2004).
[205] Gretchen Morgenson 1999. Day Trades: Big Growth, Big Risks. New York Times, July 31, Late Edition (east Coast). http://proquest.umi.com/ (accessed August 21, 2004).
[206] Joel Palmer 2000. Whom Should You Bet On? Des Moines Business Record, November 06, 13-18. http://web14.epnet.com/ (accessed August 22, 2004).
[207] John Wyatt 1996. America's amazing IPO bonanza. Fortune, May 27, 76. http://www.proquest.com/ (accessed September 6, 2004).
[208] Joseph C. Razza Jr 1993. 401(k) plans double in decade. Life Association News, December 1, 27. http://www.proquest.com/ (accessed October 31, 2007).
[209] Joseph McCafferty 1996. Endangered species. CFO, December 1, 47-54. http://www.proquest.com/ (accessed February 12, 2008).
[210] Ronald B. Lieber 1996. Who owns the 500? Fortune, April 29, 264. http://www.proquest.com/ (accessed February 14, 2008).
[211] 401(k) plans replacing traditional pensions :[ALL Edition]. 1994. Telegram & Gazette, August 29, http://www.proquest.com/ (accessed February 12, 2008).

[212] Ron Panko 2000. Employers are still satisfied with defined-benefit plans. Best's Review, January 1, 109. http://www.proquest.com/ (accessed February 14, 2008).

[213] Joseph C. Razza Jr 1993. 401(k) plans double in decade. Life Association News, December 1, 27. http://www.proquest.com/ (accessed October 31, 2007).

[214] Joseph C. Razza Jr 1993. 401(k) plans double in decade. Life Association News, December 1, 27. http://www.proquest.com/ (accessed October 31, 2007).

[215] Valerie Frazee 1996. 401(k) plans are increasingly flexible. Personnel Journal, May 1, 32. http://www.proquest.com/ (accessed February 14, 2008).

[216] Joel Palmer 2000. Whom Should You Bet On? Des Moines Business Record, November 06, 13-18. http://web14.epnet.com/ (accessed August 22, 2004).

[217] Kathleen Gallagher 1994. Growing 401(k) market getting tougher to tap. The Milwaukee Journal Sentinel, April 11, 24D. http://global.factiva.com/ha/default.aspx (accessed October 30, 2007).

[218] Joel Palmer 2000. Whom Should You Bet On? Des Moines Business Record, November 06, 13-18. http://web14.epnet.com/ (accessed August 22, 2004).

[219] Joseph McCafferty 1996. Endangered species. CFO, December 1, 47-54. http://www.proquest.com/ (accessed February 12, 2008).

[220] Joseph McCafferty 1996. Endangered species. CFO, December 1, 47-54. http://www.proquest.com/ (accessed February 12, 2008).

Chapter 7 Notes: PCs Set the Table and the Census tops it off

[221] Paul Gillin 1990. Desktop Deprivation. Computerworld: Supplement, August 13, 18. http:// proquest.umi.com/ (accessed July 31, 2004).

[222] Robert J. Samuelson 1999. The PC boom—and now bust? Newsweek, April 5, 52. http://web7.infotrac.gale-group.com/ (accessed August 1, 2004).

[223] Robert J. Samuelson 1999. The PC boom—and now bust? Newsweek, April 5, 52. http://web7.infotrac.gale-group.com/ (accessed August 1, 2004).

[224] G. Christian Hill 1995. Multi-PC homes expected to keep sales boom alive. Wall Street Journal, December 4, Eastern Edition. http://www.proquest.com/ (accessed July 31, 2004).

[225] Robert J. Samuelson 1999. The PC boom—and now bust? Newsweek, April 5, 52. http://web7.infotrac.gale-group.com/ (accessed August 1, 2004).

[226] Robert J. Samuelson 1999. The PC boom—and now bust? Newsweek, April 5, 52. http://web7.infotrac.gale-group.com/ (accessed August 1, 2004).

[227] Robert J. Samuelson 1999. The PC boom—and now bust? Newsweek, April 5, 52. http://web7.infotrac.gale-group.com/ (accessed August 1, 2004).

[228] Julie Hatch and Angela Clinton. "Job growth in the 1990s: a retrospect." Monthly Labor Review, December 2000: 3-18.

[229] Melynda Dovel Wilcox 1999. Uncle Sam's head counters want you. Kiplinger's Personal Finance Magazine, March 1, 20. http:// proquest.umi.com/ (accessed September 8, 2004).

Chapter 9 Notes: Myth Two - The Clinton Balanced Budget

[230] Bill Clinton 1995. Address to the nation on the plan to balance the budget. Weekly Compilation of Presidential Documents, June 19, 1051. http://www.proquest.com/ (accessed August 24, 2004).

[231] Unbalanced. 1995. The Economist, February 11, 27-28. http://www.proquest.com/ (accessed October 7, 2007).

[232] Steve Chapman 2001. The Legend of Bill Clinton, Budget Balancer :[Chicago Sports Final, N Edition]. Chicago Tribune, January 18. http:// proquest.umi.com/ (accessed August 23, 2004).

[233] Backtracing at the White House. 1995. U.S. News & World Report, June 5, 10. http://proquest.umi.com/ (accessed August 15, 2004).

[234] Alan Abelson 1995. Up & down Wall Street: Little Sir Echo. Barron's, June 19, 3. http://proquest.umi.com/ (accessed August 23, 2004).

[235] Howard Gleckman 1995. Bill Clinton, deficit hawk. Business Week, June 26, 36. http://proquest.umi.com/ (accessed August 23, 2004).

[236] Adam Clymer 1995. Whether friend or foe, most think Clinton is playing politics on the budget. New York Times, June 16, Late Edition (east Coast). http:// proquest.umi. com/ (accessed August 23, 2004).

[237] Hilary Stout, David Rogers. 1995. Clinton moves nearer GOP timetable to balance budget, with conditions. Wall Street Journal, October 20, Eastern Edition. http://www.proquest.com/ (accessed March 2, 2008).

[238] Alison Mitchell 1995. Clinton Attacks the G.O.P. On Priorities in Budget Plan. New York Times, July 25, Late Edition (east Coast). http://www.proquest.com/ (accessed March 2, 2008).

239 Steve Chapman 2001. The Legend of Bill Clinton, Budget Balancer :[Chicago Sports Final, N Edition]. Chicago Tribune, January 18. http:// proquest.umi.com/ (accessed August 23, 2004).

240 Don Lee 1999. Stock Options a Windfall for Workers, State Coffers; Economy: Sharp increase in volume cashed in this year boosts personal income tax revenues by $200 million :[Home Edition]. Los Angeles Times, April 24, http://www.proquest.com/ (accessed August 23, 2004).

241 Matt Krantz 2001. Stock drop hits tech-rich states; Big source of tax revenue dries up:[FINAL Edition]. USA Today, October 22, http://proquest.umi.com/ (accessed August 22, 2004).

242 Matt Krantz 2001. Stock drop hits tech-rich states; Big source of tax revenue dries up:[FINAL Edition]. USA Today, October 22, http://proquest.umi.com/ (accessed August 22, 2004).

243 David Friedman 2000. The New Soul Mates; The Stock Market's Latest Convert: Government :[Home Edition]. Los Angeles Times, May 7, http://proquest.umi.com/ (accessed August 22, 2004).

244 David Friedman 2000. The New Soul Mates; The Stock Market's Latest Convert: Government :[Home Edition]. Los Angeles Times, May 7, http://proquest.umi.com/ (accessed August 22, 2004).

245 David Friedman 2000. The New Soul Mates; The Stock Market's Latest Convert: Government :[Home Edition]. Los Angeles Times, May 7, http://proquest.umi.com/ (accessed August 22, 2004).

246 Merrill Goozner 1998. Rich Investors Fill U.S. Coffers Income Inequality Pays Off in Taxes; [North Sports Final Edition]. Chicago Tribune, April 11. http:// proquest.umi. com/ (accessed August 23, 2004).

247 Kimberly Blanton, Globe Staff 2000. "AMERICANS' ARDOR FOR STOCK UNSHAKEN BY MARKET

VOLATILITY INVESTORS PUT RECORD $54 BILLION IN EQUITY MUTUAL FUNDS IN FEBRUARY." Boston Globe. April 8, C1. http://proquest. umi.com/ (accessed August 22, 2004).

[248] George Hager 1999. No `April Surprise' in Store for Federal Budget This Year :[FINAL Edition]. The Washington Post, April 30, http://www.proquest.com/ (accessed August 22, 2004).

[249] Rone Tempest 2000. California and the West; Surplus Gives State Choices in Spending; Economics: Proliferating dot-coms and stock options will provide extra billions. Schools, infrastructure or tax cuts could be funded :[Home Edition]. Los Angeles Times, January 31, http://www.proquest.com/ (accessed August 23, 2004).

[250] Peter G. Gosselin 2002. THE NATION; Lower Tax Receipts Could Double U.S. Budget Deficit; Revenue: A shortfall is likely, but administration officials say there's still time to reverse the trend :[HOME EDITION]. Los Angeles Times, April 26, http://www.proquest.com/ (accessed August 22, 2004).

Chapter 10 Notes: Myth Three - Bill Clinton the Welfare Reformer

[251] Richard E. Cohen 1994. Welfare reform's obstacle course. National Journal, May 14, 1150. http://www.proquest.com/ (accessed September 3, 2007).

[252] Elizabeth Shogren 1996. Welfare Impasse Forces States to Craft Own Plans :[Home Edition]. Los Angeles Times (pre-1997 Fulltext), April 15, http://www.proquest.com/ (accessed March 29, 2008).

[253] Robert Dole, William F. Weld. 1996. States know best on welfare reform :[ALL Edition]. Telegram & Gazette, March 7, http://www.proquest.com/ (accessed March 25, 2008).

[254] David Finkel 1996. Michigan's "Welfare Reform". Against the Current, March 1, 28. http://www.proquest.com/ (accessed March 25, 2008).

[255] Elizabeth Shogren 1996. Welfare Impasse Forces States to Craft Own Plans :[Home Edition]. Los Angeles Times (pre-1997 Fulltext), April 15, http://www.proquest.com/ (accessed March 29, 2008).

[256] Robert L. Jackson 1996. Clinton Praises GOP Governor's Welfare Model :[Home Edition]. Los Angeles Times (pre-1997 Fulltext), May 19, http://www.proquest.com/ (accessed March 29, 2008).

[257] Barbara Vobejda 1996. Welfare Bill Glides Through Senate; Approval Sends Overhaul to White House for Clinton Signature :[FINAL Edition]. The Washington Post (pre-1997 Fulltext), August 2, http://www.proquest.com/ (accessed March 25, 2008).

[258] Barbara Vobejda 1996. Welfare Bill Glides Through Senate; Approval Sends Overhaul to White House for Clinton Signature :[FINAL Edition]. The Washington Post (pre-1997 Fulltext), August 2, http://www.proquest.com/ (accessed March 25, 2008).

Chapter 11 Notes: Selected Policy Issues Where Clinton Was "Out in Front"

[259] Jodie T. Allen 1994. CBO's Necessary Operation;The Price of Doctoring the Health Numbers :[FINAL Edition]. The Washington Post (pre-1997 Fulltext), February 13, http://global.factiva.com/ (accessed December 27, 2007).

[260] Blow to Clinton's Healthcare Reforms - CBO Says Plan Would be Drain on Budget. 1994. Financial Times, February 17, http://global.factiva.com/ (accessed December 25, 2007).

[261] Blow to Clinton's Healthcare Reforms - CBO Says Plan Would be Drain on Budget. 1994. Financial Times, February 17, http://global.factiva.com/ (accessed December 25, 2007).

[262] Actuaries examine Clinton plan numbers. 1993. Employee Benefit Plan Review, December 1, 46. http://www.proquest.com/ (accessed December 27, 2007).

[263] Clinton's plan: DOA? 1994. Time, February 14, 20. http://global.factiva.com/ (accessed December 25, 2007).

[264] Clinton's plan: DOA? 1994. Time, February 14, 20. http://global.factiva.com/ (accessed December 25, 2007).

[265] Richard L. Clarke 1994. Healthcare reform: Now what? Healthcare Financial Management, November 1, 12. http://www.proquest.com/ (accessed December 25, 2007).

[266] James Risen, William J. Eaton. 1993. GOP Senator Offers Job Bill Compromise Budget: Hatfield proposes slicing at least $7 billion off Clinton's $16.3-billion economic stimulus package. No sign yet of an agreement :[Home Edition]. Los Angeles Times (pre-1997 Fulltext), April 20, http://www.proquest.com/ (accessed March 16, 2008).

267 Jeffrey H. Birnbaum and David Rogers 1993. Clinton Pursues Strategy to Pass Stimulus Bill — President Lambastes GOP While Aides Reach Out To Gain Needed Votes. Wall Street Journal, April 13, Eastern Edition. http://www.proquest.com/ (accessed March 16, 2008).

268 James Risen, William J. Eaton. 1993. GOP Senator Offers Job Bill Compromise Budget: Hatfield proposes slicing at least $7 billion off Clinton's $16.3-billion economic stimulus package. No sign yet of an agreement :[Home Edition]. Los Angeles Times (pre-1997 Fulltext), April 20, http://www.proquest.com/ (accessed March 16, 2008).

269 Stephen A. Davies 1993. Hard Knocks and Some Uninspiring Figures Start Chipping the Administration's Paint Job. Bond Buyer, April 19, http://www.proquest.com/ (accessed March 16, 2008).

270 Stephen Barr 1993. Reorganization Report Goes to Clinton Today :[FINAL Edition]. The Washington Post (pre-1997 Fulltext), September 7, http://www.proquest.com/ (accessed December 29, 2007).

271 Clinton and Gore Unveil Reinventing Government Plan. 1993. All Things Considered September 7 1. http://www.proquest.com/ (accessed December 29, 2007).

272 Stephen Barr 1994. Celebrating Progress in `Reinvention'; At South Lawn Ceremony, Clinton Hails Gore Initiative's First Year :[FINAL Edition]. The Washington Post (pre-1997 Fulltext), September 15, http://www.proquest.com/ (accessed December 29, 2007).

273 Brad Stratton 1997. Four more years of reinventing government. Quality Progress 30, no. 3 (March 1): 45-46+. http://www.proquest.com/ (accessed December 29, 2007).

274 William H. Miller 1994. Reinventing government: The ultimate management challenge. Industry Week,

November 7, 65. http://www.proquest.com/ (accessed December 29, 2007).

275 William H. Miller 1994. Reinventing government: The ultimate management challenge. Industry Week, November 7, 65. http://www.proquest.com/ (accessed December 29, 2007).

276 William H. Miller 1994. Reinventing government: The ultimate management challenge. Industry Week, November 7, 65. http://www.proquest.com/ (accessed December 29, 2007).

277 William H. Miller 1994. Reinventing government: The ultimate management challenge. Industry Week, November 7, 65. http://www.proquest.com/ (accessed December 29, 2007).

278 Stephen Barr 1998. After 5 Years, Gore's Reinvention Gets a `B'; Brookings Analyst Says Results Vary Widely :[FINAL Edition]. The Washington Post, September 4, http://www.proquest.com/ (accessed December 29, 2007).

279 Brad Stratton 1997. Four more years of reinventing government. Quality Progress 30, no. 3 (March 1): 45-46+. http://www.proquest.com/ (accessed December 29, 2007).

280 Stephen Barr 1994. Celebrating Progress in `Reinvention'; At South Lawn Ceremony, Clinton Hails Gore Initiative's First Year :[FINAL Edition]. The Washington Post (pre-1997 Fulltext), September 15, http://www.proquest.com/ (accessed December 29, 2007).

Chapter 12 Notes: Lessons Learned from the '90s Economic Boom

[281] Daniel J. Lyons 1989. PCs fuel economic growth, accelerate shift to service jobs. PC Week, December 25, 89. http://www.proquest.com/ (accessed December 28, 2007).

[282] Glen Dickson 2007. Nielsen Gives Fuzzy Picture of HDTV Penetration. Broadcasting & Cable, November 5, 5. http://www.proquest.com/ (accessed January 14, 2008).

[283] Kevin Downey 2005. The HDTV Revolution Takes Its Time. Broadcasting & Cable, May 30, 30. http://www.proquest.com/ (accessed January 11, 2008).

[284] The changing face of research. 2005. Managing Intellectual Property, December 1, 6. http://www.proquest.com/ (accessed January 6, 2008).

[285] The changing face of research. 2005. Managing Intellectual Property, December 1, 7. http://www.proquest.com/ (accessed January 6, 2008).

[286] The changing face of research. 2005. Managing Intellectual Property, December 1, 6. http://www.proquest.com/ (accessed January 6, 2008).

[287] Science and Technology: Bayhing for blood or Doling out cash?; Intellectual property. 2005. The Economist, December 24, 115. http://www.proquest.com/ (accessed January 6, 2008).

[288] The changing face of research. 2005. Managing Intellectual Property, December 1, 2. http://www.proquest.com/ (accessed January 6, 2008).

[289] The changing face of research. 2005. Managing Intellectual Property, December 1, 3. http://www.proquest.com/ (accessed January 6, 2008).

[290] Science and Technology: Bayhing for blood or Doling out cash?; Intellectual property. 2005. The Economist,

December 24, 115. http://www.proquest.com/ (accessed January 6, 2008).

291 Science and Technology: Bayhing for blood or Doling out cash?; Intellectual property. 2005. The Economist, December 24, 115. http://www.proquest.com/ (accessed January 6, 2008).

292 "Manhattan Project." www.wikipedia.org. April 15, 2008. http://en.wikipedia.org/wiki/The_Manhattan_Project (accessed April 15, 2008).

293 Robert Crandall, Jerry Ellig 1997. Economic Deregulation and Customer Choice: Lessons for the Electric Industry. Mercatus Center at George Mason University. January 1. http://www.mercatus.org/repository/docLib/MC_RSP_RP-Dregulation_970101.pdf (accessed October 27, 2007).

294 Robert Crandall, Jerry Ellig 1997. Economic Deregulation and Customer Choice: Lessons for the Electric Industry. Mercatus Center at George Mason University. January 1. http://www.mercatus.org/repository/docLib/MC_RSP_RP-Dregulation_970101.pdf (accessed October 27, 2007).

295 James M. Pethokoukis 2006. Jobs Boost. U.S. News & World Report, July 17, 51. http://www.proquest.com/ (accessed April 7, 2008).

296 Cisco Systems. "Financial Review - Notes to Consolidated Financial Statements - Annual Report 2000 - Cisco Systems." www.cisco.com. 2000. http://www.cisco.com/web/about/ac49/ac20/ac19/ar2000/financials/ncfs.html (accessed April 15, 2008).

297 Cisco Systems. "Financial Review - Notes to Consolidated Financial Statements - Annual Report 2004 - Cisco Systems." www.cisco.com. 2005. http://www.cisco.com/web/about/ac49/ac20/ac19/ar2004/financial_review/ncfs.html (accessed April 15, 2008).